ANOTHER TIME ANOTHER PLACE

A nostalgic and humorous look at life in St. John's
during the 1940s and 1950s

by
Jack Fitzgerald

ANOTHER TIME
ANOTHER PLACE

A nostalgic and humorous look at life in St. John's
during the 1940s and 1950s

by
Jack Fitzgerald

Creative Book Publishing
St. John's, Newfoundland
1997

Appreciation is expressed to *The Canada Council* for publication assistance.

Cover: Maurice Fitzgerald

∝ Printed on acid-free paper

Published by
CREATIVE BOOK PUBLISHING
a division of 10366 Newfoundland Limited
a Robinson-Blackmore Printing & Publishing associated company
P.O. Box 8660, St. John's, Newfoundland A1B 3T7

First printing, January 1997
Second printing, April 1998

Printed in Canada by:
ROBINSON-BLACKMORE PRINTING & PUBLISHING

Canadian Cataloguing in Publication Data

Fitzgerald, Jack, 1945-

    Another time, another place

    ISBN 1-895387-75-2

1. St. John's (Nfld.) — Social life and customs.   I. Title.
FC2196.394.F57   1997   971.8'104   C96-950241-9

Dedication

I dedicate this book to the memory of my late brother Maurice Fitzgerald. He was very much a part of my childhood and I treasure some wonderful memories of our relationship. His sudden death in 1961 while only 21 years old left a void in my life that has never been filled.

Table of Contents

Foreword

Another Time-Another Place is a nostalgic and sometimes humorous look, at life in downtown St. John's, during the last years of Newfoundland as a British Colony, and the first years as a province of Canada.

St. John's, the capital city of Britain's oldest colony, was like another country when compared with the St. John's of today — the capital of Canada's newest province.

Not only did people socialize differently but the physical aspects were quite different. We had no network of highways to connect our cities, towns, and communities. Instead, Newfoundlanders relied on the railway and the sea for transportation. In cities and small communities the automobile had not come into its own and horses were still being used for transportation.

In St. John's, only the major thoroughfares had been paved. The dusty streets motivated people to paint their homes dull colours. We had none of the variety of bright colours seen today. Instead, there was row after row of mostly red and green structures with the odd grey or brown.

People kept animals within the city. There were many stables around the city to house horses used by the business community for deliveries. Chicken coops in back gardens were also common. Some families kept chicken and turkey in these coops.

Water and sewerage were luxuries and the nightly visit of the honey wagon on city streets was an accepted part of life. Supermarkets were unheard of — and people gathered their groceries from multiple sources. These sources included corner grocery stores, butcher shops and the door to door vendors. Every Saturday an army of wagons ladened down with fresh produce from the little villages outside the city descended upon St. John's and peddled vegetables, meats and berries door to door.

Those of us who grew up in the 1940s and 1950s experienced a way of life that will never be repeated. We were the last generation of Newfoundlanders in Britain's oldest colony and we were the first generation of children to experience life in the same city as a province of Canada.

Looking back on those days is like looking back at a foreign country and an entirely different way of life. Our playgrounds were the dusty, unpaved streets, meadows and fields of St. John's that have long since been turned into housing or commercial developments.

We used imagination and ingenuity to provide our own recreation and spending money. We played in the horse stables and on the jetty wharfs of the old harbour front. We cut seal meat, shovelled coal and sold splits and bottles to earn pocket money.

We lived in houses built for the 19th century, most with no water and sewerage, poorly insulated and in today's society would be considered unbearably cold in wintertime.

We lived in a time when disease and malnutrition were common and most people couldn't afford even the basic cost of a doctor's visit. Home remedies often sufficed for medical treatment or prescriptions. I was born in the back-room of 35 Flower Hill with only a mid-wife in attendance. Mid-wives and home births were common.

Despite the adversity and hardships experienced most of us recall our childhood downtown as a memorable and happy experience.

A defining characteristic of the era was the people. The way of life contributed to neighbours being closer, friendlier and supportive to each other. The bonds of friendship which developed in those times have lasted a life time for most.

Even today people who grew up downtown will stop others whom they only knew casually, or were familiar faces in that era and say "I can't remember the name...but I know the f - - k'n face. Then they will engage in hours of nostalgic recollections of a treasured place in our past.

In this book, I attempted to recreate a glimpse of that era, its hardships, its oddities and its humour. I hope that you enjoy reading *Another Time, Another Place* as much as I enjoyed writing it.

Acknowledgements

I am grateful to a number of people for their help and encouragement in writing this book. I thank my friend Jack Murphy for his encouragment. For years he has been pressuring me to write about our downtown neighbourhood of the 40s and 50s. I finally gave in and did it. Special thanks to Bob Rumsey and Frank Galgay for their support and guidance. Several friends were kind enough to read the manuscript before I submitted it for publication to test public reaction. Their response and encouragment convinced me the book could have wide appeal. For this I thank, Helen Stephens, Brian and Tom Healy, Jean Murphy, Phil Leonard, Richard Hartery, Joan Pope and Pat Hearn. I thank all my old friends for the time they shared with me in recalling our earlier lives. A special thanks to all those who allowed me to borrow family pictures. For this I thank, Al Smith, Alan Hatcher, Rick Harris, Jim Walsh, Frank and Jean Murphy, Frank and Rose Jackman.

A very special thanks to my god son, Jeff Earle for posing for the front cover drawing and several pictures. I am most grateful to Don Morgan of Creative Book Publishing for his patience, guidance and support in preparing this manuscript for publication. In closing I thank my son Maurice for his creative talent and artistic ability in designing the front cover which captures an era now frozen in many of our memories.

Child's Life

"I got a bogger on you!"

Bouncer Abbott leaped over the water tank on the corner of Flower Hill and Central Street, making the announcement that would begin the game of "boggers," take us all over town, and end up with a policeman splashing around in St. John's Harbour.

Boggers was a game where the leader would perform a challenging feat—climb a fence, jump a fire hydrant, hit a streetlight with a stone. The followers would have to do the same or drop out.

Jumping over the water tank was no easy feat, but one by one, like chicks parading behind a mother hen, we followed Bouncer: Charlie Fowler, Frankey Whelan, Jackie Murphy, Richard (Dickie) Murphy, Beaver Murphy, Maurice Fitzgerald and, last but not least, myself.

By the time my turn came to jump over the water tank, Bouncer had led the gang to the concrete wall beside Walsh's Bakery on Central Street. The new bogger was to jump from the wall five feet down into the field below. But I was still stuck getting over the hydrant. I knew I couldn't do it, but I didn't want to be knocked out so early in the game. So, with the others all following the leader and no one looking back, I

Courtesy: Al Smith

Waterfront playground: Children found excitement and danger on the old waterfront. This picture shows the waterfront in 1958. This area is now the parking lot behind the Scotia Centre on Water Street.

jumped in the air to make a landing sound, grunted, and ran to catch up with the boys. Dickie Murphy had just jumped the wall. I followed. And the boggers went on as we jig-sawed in and out of the downtown streets until finally we were at the harbour front.

The harbour of 1951 was very different than today. The great reconstruction of the harbour front was not even dreamed of. There was no harbour front road. The backs of the Water Street stores faced the harbour and from each store property a wharf jetted out into the harbour. Many small boats tied up at these wharfs, some owned by city fishermen who sold their catch from Steer's Wharf. The area was a popular place for boggers, especially for the challenge of jumping from one boat to another.

Maybe this was why our parents made plain we were to avoid the waterfront. Every so often we would hear of a boy drowning while playing in the area, but we felt safe enough that day. We were confident that there was safety in numbers.

Constable Coady was walking the beat that day. When he heard the sound of a boy crying at the wharf he ran down the laneway to investigate. Richard Murphy was standing at the side of the wharf bawling his lungs out. He was pointing to a hat floating in the water and stuttering, "My, br... br... brother, my br... .br... brother!"

Before anyone could explain anything, Coady kicked off his boots, tossed his hat aside and dove into the harbour waters. He swam to the hat then submerged. Up he would come and back again beneath the surface over and over. Finally, he shouted to Richard, "Where did your brother fall in?" Richard answered, "No, ... my brother ... my brother ... he threw my hat in the water!"

We didn't need Bouncer to lead us at that point. Everyone started scrambling ... up the laneway, across Water Street in and out of alleyways, gardens and fields until we got to our houses.

Richard 'Dickie' Murphy: When he lost his hat in the harbour it caused a policeman to take a dunk in the harbour waters. Picture was taken on Flower Hill in June 1959. Dickie is wearing his Holy Cross uniform, ready to participate in the Annual Holy Cross Sports Day.

At ages ten to twelve we respected and feared the police on the beat. Certainly, we did not relish the thought of being brought home by the collar by a policeman. Unfortunately, Richard didn't get away. Coady, grabbed him by the collar and marched him to his house on Flower Hill. He got his hat back . . . but he also a got few whacks of the broom across the rear end when his mother learned he had been down on the wharf. In our case, my brother and I also got a taste of the broomstick. It was quite some time before I followed Bouncer or anyone else in another game of boggers.

Some of our friends were far more daring and adventurous when playing on the waterfront. Just a few days after Richard enticed Coady into the harbour waters, our friends Ike and Al Smith from New Gower Street, two boys both under eleven years old, faced a real life-threatening situation.

The Smith brothers decided to take a row around the harbour in one of the fishing dories tied up at Steer's Wharf. Al untied the boat and pushed her away from the wharf while Ike positioned the two oars. Neither one had rowed a boat before but they were willing to learn. Several of their friends beckoned for them to return to shore but the two boys ignored them. After some zig zagging along the waters they finally got the little craft under control and began rowing towards the Narrows.

Anyone who has ventured in a boat on the harbour and out through the Narrows know only too well how different the waters can be inside and outside the Narrows. This was one of those days. Neither Al nor Ike had any idea of what to expect. The harbour waters were relatively calm. However, when they got to the Narrows two events occurred that put the fear of God into them and frightened those watching from shore.

First, Ike dropped one of the oars into the water and they were having trouble retrieving it. Then suddenly the waters changed from calm to rough and the little dory began tossing around and out of control. Al managed to guide the missing oar close enough to the dory to grab hold of. Although very young and in a threatening situation, they kept cool and concentrated their efforts on getting the boat to shore. They headed for a wharf near Temperance Street in the east end of St. John's where, to the delight of their friends, they made it safely to shore.

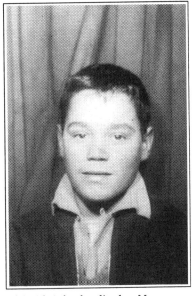

Al Smith (who then lived on New Gower Street) tried to row out the harbour in 1953.

Episodes like this were not unusual in those days when many children turned to the waterfront for play and adventure.

Living in downtown St. John's in the late 1940s and early 1950s was like living in a foreign country when compared to the city of today. The streets were dusty and unpaved. Because of the dust around the city, home owners avoided bright paint on their houses. House colours in the city were limited to three: red, green and grey. Some houses showed no paint whatsover, because it had long worn off and people couldn't afford to repaint it. It wasn't unusual to come across rows of unpainted houses with the clapboards falling off or missing.

Most houses did not have running water and many no electricity. Water was obtained from water tanks like the one at which we started our game of boggers. These tanks were iron sculptures, with a lion's head with open mouth from which the water gushed. Every neighbourhood had its own water tank. These tanks were instrumental in people of the neighbourhood getting to know each other. On a daily basis people would line up at the water tanks with their buckets, and on wash days there would be repeated trips to get enough water to wash the family clothes.

Every home had its drinking water bucket and dipper which was used to scoop up the water when the need arose to satisfy a thirst. A dipper was like a miniature saucepan. You would fill the dipper with water from the bucket, take a drink, and pass it around to others awaiting refreshment. If you were outside playing you would drink from the water tank by placing your mouth over the tank spout and pulling the handle. You could squirt the water at people standing nearby by plugging the outlet with your finger, and kids frequently did this.

Every family had a galvanized wash tub which would be used as a clothes washer on wash day, usually Monday, and as a bath tub on Saturday's. Sunlight soap was the universal soap of the working class. It was used to wash the clothing, wash the children and to scrub the front steps. Yes . . . for some reason it seemed important that the front steps to each house be scrubbed clean.

Saturday night was the accepted time for the weekly tub bath. The streets would be eerily cleared of children at an early hour. If you were not home for the scrub one of your parents would be out looking for you. One tub of water washed all the children. Getting hot water for bathing was not an easy task especially when there were several children lined up waiting for a scrubbing. Hot water for the wash had to be drawn from the tank and boiled in pots on the stove. So, if you were the youngest in a large family the water was very discoloured by the time your turn came. Sunlight soap was scrubbed over your body and into your scalp. It was common to hear children bawling when the harsh soap got into their eyes. Following, the scrub, you would be given a going over with a fine-tooth comb to make sure your head was clean. During the week you washed daily from a pan of water. A porcelain bowl and jug were common in many homes for this purpose. The jug was always kept filled with water usually taken from the bucket of water which was the family drinking supply. When needed, this water was poured into the bowl for washing purposes.

During the 1950s there were two very popular styles of hair cuts for boys. The crew cut, also called the GI because the military used it, was popular in summertime because the barber left very little hair on your head. The hair was cut close and stood up like the bristles of a brush. Instead of combing you had to brush it each day to keep it in appropriate form. The other style was the DA, or "duck's ass," made popular by Elvis Presley. You needed a good head of hair to have a DA. To style and form the hair into the DA we used Brylcreme or Vaseline. Both gave the hair a very greasy look, but Vaseline would keep it in place for days. It also gathered a lot of dirt which stuck to it and accumulated. Washing this grease out of your hair was not an easy task.

Getting water for a wash was not the only way in which life was different from today. Back then, there were frequent tea breaks to socialize with neighbours who often dropped in to visit and chat. When special visitors or guests dropped by, the table cloth would be taken from its storage place and placed over the table, and special china would be used for serving tea. No such thing then as tea bags. Every home had a kettle, tea pot and tea strainer. They would brew the tea by scooping tea leaves into a tea pot and adding hot water.

While the tea steeped they would boil a kettle of water. "Do you want your tea weak or strong?" you would be asked. A weak cup of tea would be about a quarter cup of strained tea from the tea pot with boiling water from the kettle added. For a stronger cup you added more tea from the pot. The strainer, a metal mesh with a handle, was placed over the cup as the tea was being poured and would stop the tea leaves from going into the cup. There was always someone in the neighbourhood who claimed to read the tea leaves. This was done by turning the cup upside down after drinking the tea. A few tea leaves always got into a cup. Turned upside down, the leaves would form a variety of patterns. The reader of the tea leaves would interpret these patterns to tell your future.

A slice of toast was made very differently than it is today, and tasted much better. Toast was made at the grate of the stove or on top of the stove. To make toast at the grate, you would put a fork through the bread and press the bread against the grate. The fork would hold it in place. When it began to smoke, you would remove the fork, turn the bread upside down and put the fork in again to return the bread to the grate until smoke appeared once more. Toast usually had a burnt flavour, but it was a memorable taste. Some people used wire contraptions on top of the stove to toast bread. We often made these from clothes hangers. These items would stand on the stove and you would place the bread around them. Once again, smoke arising from the bread would mean it was done. Caplin could also be roasted this way.

Toast was not the only food that would smoke when ready. One lady on the street whom I will call Nell was considered by most people to be a lousy cook. Yet she devised a sure-fire way to cook a roast for Sunday dinner. She would buy two roasts, a large one and a small one. Nell would place both in the oven, and when the little one burned up, the big one was done.

Nobody had fridges. In the summer time the ice man would come with a truck load of broken ice which sold for ten cents a jug. How he got the ice in the first place is an intriguing piece of old city trivia. The ice man was a Mr. Tom Burke. During the winter months he cut huge slabs of ice from Kent's Pond or Burton's Pond, stored it in an unrefrigerated warehouse and covered it with sawdust. The sawdust kept the ice from melting during hot weather. In the summertime he would load a pickup truck with the ice and sell it door to door. The arrival of the iceman in a neighbourhood on a hot summer's day was welcomed by everyone, especially the kids. We tagged behind the ice man, and whenever he left the truck unattended to make a sale we would climb up the back, grab a junk of ice and scram.

Very few people owned a car in those days. I remember well the curiosity a car aroused when it parked somewhere in the neighbourhood. Adults questioned who owned it and the kids marvelled at it. My own inquisitiveness about the automobile nearly got me killed when I was only three years old. What seemed to me to be a huge black car parked on Flower Hill directly across the street from where I was playing. The sound of the claxton horn captivated me. Ahh-ooo-ga! ... Ahh-ooo-ga! I felt compelled to investigate the sound so I toddled across the street and walked all round the car viewing and touching it from every angle.

The driver, a tall man in a dark suit, got out and went into a nearby house. I sat down on the car's runner, a metal strip around twelve to-fifteen inches wide which ran along the car on both sides from the front door to the back. This was used as a step for people entering or leaving the vehicle. To me, at age three, it looked more like a seat or a bench. I sat on it. I had long light brown curly hair which was nearly the cause of my undoing.

I paid little attention to the sound of the door opening and closing on the driver's side. Nor was I distracted by the sound of the car starting. The driver had not noticed me sitting on the runner and he accelerated. The jerking motion tossed me to the ground but my long hair became entangled in the runner and the

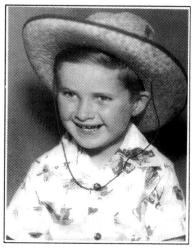

Author Jack Fitzgerald: This picture was taken several months after he was dragged by a car on Flower Hill.

moving car dragged me with it. Fortunately, Rose Murphy (Rose Jackman today) was standing near Fardy's Store and saw what was happening.

Rose ran after the car shouting to the top of her lungs for the driver to stop. He heard her and brought the vehicle to a sudden stop. Meanwhile, the car had travelled forty or fifty feet with me bouncing around on the unpaved, stone-spotted, dusty hill. Blood was running from my head when Rose picked me up in her arms and brought me to my mother. My arms and legs were cut, bruised and scraped as well.

The driver suggested he take me to St. Clare's Hospital for medical attention. The blood from my head was caused by the hair that had been pulled out. Apart from some bruises and scratches it appeared I was not seriously injured. Dr. Tolson Smith, our family doctor, came to my home later that evening and cautioned my mother to watch for signs of concussion. There was no concussion and I soon recovered.

Bread wagons: Delivery wagons load up at Walsh's Bakery on Central Street. The horse on the far left was a one time racer in the famous Kentucky Derby. Moses H. Walsh raced her locally.

For several years after that I had a very different feeling about the call of the Ahh-000-ga!

In those days there were far more horses in use than cars. Walsh's Bakery had a barn on Flower Hill which housed their fleet of five or six horses and wagons. I remember as a very young boy going along with John and Jerry Walsh (grandsons of Skipper Walsh, owner of Walsh's Bakery) whenever they brought the stable's pony to the blacksmith to be shod. To have a horse shod meant to have new horseshoes put on him and the old ones removed. We found the process fascinating.

The blacksmith always had a red hot fire going and there was the constant ringing and clanging of metal hitting metal and the spectacular spraying of bright hot sparks into the air as the blacksmith carved hooves and shaped iron into shoes for the horse. Then he would remove the old worn out ones by pulling the small nails that held them in place on the horse's hoof. The new ones would be nailed in place by the blacksmith and then we were off again.

There were many blacksmiths around town, but on this occasion we went to one in the Fleming Street area. It was a real adventure for us to be alone with a pony which we could easily imagine was Roy Roger's horse 'Trigger' or Gene Autrey's 'Champion'. Which one we chose to imagine depended on who was holding the reins. On this occasion we decided to do something we had not tried before—ride the pony. The pony was not wearing a saddle and I had no idea then, that it was very difficult riding bareback.

In fact, for an inexperienced six-year-old it was damn impossible. I learned this lesson the hard way. Jerry, the eldest of our trio by a year or two, set out the distance for each of us to ride. He took the first ride from Fleming Street to St. Pat's School on Merrymeeting Road. At that point he invited me, over John's objections, to take the second ride from St. Pat's to Parade Street. I should have let John take the ride, but I felt it was an easy task. After all, every Saturday at the York Theatre we witnessed cowboys of all ages riding horses and it looked so effortless. Jerry and John helped me onto the pony's back.

Jerry ordered me to "Hold onto her mane!" I spent enough time with Jerry and John at their barn to know the horse's mane was the long hair running down over the back of her head. I seized the mane and felt pretty important as the pony slowly paced herself along Merrymeeting Road. We hadn't gone twenty-five feet when Jerry let go the reins and whipped the pony with the branch of a tree he had picked up near St. Pat's. It's funny how swiftly fun can turn into terror.

I was absolutely terrorized as the pony broke into a gallop

and I was clinging to her neck for dear life. Up and down ... up and down ... side to side. I was being tossed all over the pony and screaming "... help, help!" I remember hearing Jerry shout "Whoa, Trigger ... Whoa Trigger !" I was no Roy Rogers by a long shot. We had planned on turning down Parade Street but there was no stopping or turning this Trigger. We zipped passed Parade Street and I was still screaming and bouncing around on the out-of-control galloping pony. A man working in the building now occupied by Clar Janes Service Station saw that I was in trouble and ran out into the street to stop the pony.

It was too late for me. Just before he got the pony under control I was tossed into the air and somersaulted onto the street. John and Jerry caught up to us and Jerry took control of Trigger. When I got to my feet I was delighted just to be conscious. But the ride had taken its toll on me. It was my first and last ride on any of the Walsh's horses, saddled or not. When I got home I was in agony. My right side felt like it was on fire. I removed my shirt and pants and panicked when I saw that most of my stomach and side was purple. My mother assured me that it was only bruised and there was no need to worry.

The following summer I learned another lesson about horses. Never stand behind them when they are eating. Jerry, John and I took one of the delivery horses up to Caul's Field to graze. Caul's Field was the site now occupied by Cabot Apartments. Michael (Dinty) Hearn was playing ball with some of the boys from Flower Hill. He came over and asked Jerry if he could ride the horse. Although Jerry was knowledgeable about horses he chose to have some fun rather than to enlighten us. I was standing behind the grazing horse when Dinty seized its mane and attempted to pull himself onto her back. It was a lesson for both of us. The horse went wild. She jumped, knocking Dinty on his rear end. As she jumped, she kicked backward, connecting with me and sending me arse over kettle.

The lessons we learned that day were: never attempt to mount a horse when she is eating, and never, never, never stand behind a grazing horse when someone is trying to mount it. After that I avoided Jerry and the horses. Whenever I went to the barn with John we played in the wagons housed adjacent to the stables.

Jim Walsh, son of Skipper, also learned a valuable lesson about dealing with horses one cold February day. His father had just added two Shetland Ponies to his stable. One was a black and white pony with one side almost all white and the other side black. After inspecting them Skipper noticed the white side of the black and white pony was dirty. Skipper instructed Jim, then in his early teens, to get a bucket of water from Mrs. Hipditch who lived adjacent to the barn and clean up the horse. ‘

Jim loved horses and especially the ponies. He delighted in the task and after satisfying himself that the white side of the pony was clean decided to give her a good scrubbing. Jim went to his father and told him the job was finished and the pony was as clean as a whistle.

The next morning when Skipper Walsh went to the barn to inspect the horses, the pony was lying dead on the floor, frozen like a popsicle. Jimmy never again washed a pony or horse during winter frost.

Horse drawn carts were also used to deliver coal for the kitchen stoves, groceries, and shop supplies to the corner grocery stores. I recall many occasions when horses with coal deliveries could not make it up Flower Hill. We became so attuned to the problem of a horse being forced to carry too much weight that we would gather by Jim Fardy's store and bet on whether or not the coal carts would make it to the top of the hill. If they couldn't make it the driver would whip the horse and try to force her to keep moving. Sometimes the whip did the trick. But most often not, and the driver would have to turn around and go back to the coal company to unload some of his cargo.

A tiny Chinaman named Joey was well known to everyone by his first name only. He collected shirts for his laundry in a little wagon drawn by a single horse. For just ten cents his laundry washed the shirts and starched the collars and cuffs. Joey tossed all the shirts collected into a large blue cloth bag and tossed the bag into the wagon. To this day, its still a mystery as to how Joey was able to return the shirts to their correct owners.

Once while the horse and wagon was tied to a light pole on Flower Hill, Gus Murphy untied the horse got on its back and took off over Central Street singing "Hi Ho Silver," the cry of the Lone Ranger. He was singing a different tune when Harry, his father got him home.

On another occasion, Gus and Tucker Crotty tied Joey to a catamaran on top of Flower Hill and let it go uncontrolled down over the hill. The only words we could understand as the contraption sailed passed Fardy's Store near Central Street was, "... little bastards." Joey went without mishap until he came to the bottom of the hill and collided with Miss Pender's gallery. He broke an arm and for the next few weeks had to manoeuvre around to his customers using one arm to guide his horse, while the other remained in a cast.

Occasionally a horse would run wild through the city and we had our share of people being run over by horses. If a horse fell and broke his leg he was shot on the spot. For a lover of animals like myself this was a dreadful spectacle to witness. I remember one incident when a horse ran wild from Cabot

Street to the corner of Monroe and Flower Hill where the wagon she was strapped to tipped over and she fell breaking a leg. I recall standing among the crowd looking on helplessly at the suffering animal. A man was called in to put the animal out of its misery. He had a large sledge hammer but I didn't understand how he was going to kill the horse. The adults in the crowd made all the children get away and out of sight. We went back to the corner of Central and Flower Hill but our eyes froze on the crowd surrounding the injured horse. We heard its last neigh ... and then a loud crackling sound like the firing of a gun, followed by silence. Then came a sight I have never forgotten: blood flowing down the drain that ran down the side of Flower Hill. We didn't completely understand why, but we knew the horse had been killed.

But most of my experience of horses, after that one wild pony ride, was confined to the movies. The York Theatre, located on Water Street opposite Parker and Monroe Shoe Stores, was a popular place for kids growing up in downtown St. John's during the 1940s and 1950s. As a matter of fact all the theatres played a big part in the lives of city kids during this period. Television did not arrive until 1955, fast food take outs were unheard of, and every place in town, including the corner candy stores, closed down on Sundays. Theatres had no food concessions so we brought our own food into the movies. The Princess Confectionery store next to the York was always a busy place before a matinee with kids stocking up for the movie.

Children's heroes of that era were a far cry from todays Ninja Turtles and Power Rangers. Our heroes were cowboys like Roy Rogers, Gene Autrey, Hopalong Cassidy, Buck Jones, The Lone Ranger and a host of others. Then there was Tarzan, Jungle Jim, Super Man, Batman and Captain Marvel. It seems in retrospect that every Saturday we could count on

Magnificent stage of the York: Before becoming the York, this theatre was named the Queen's, and was frequently used for local live entertainment. The late Don Jamieson once performed on stage there.

at least one of the city's movie theatres featuring one of the above. In addition to the weekly feature movie there were the weekly serials or cliff hangers which seemed to never end. To follow one of the serials you had to keep coming back to the same theatre.

Just down the street from the York on the opposite side was the Crescent Theatre owned by the Boulous family. That theatre burned down around 1948 or 1949. It was in the area later occupied by Woolworth's or a little further down. Because it was constructed near a harbour wharf, the Crescent was known best for its sea smells of salty water and fresh fish. Regardless of the fishy smells, the Crescent was popular. The close proximity to the salt water with all its bouquets added an extra layer of realism to a sea movie like *Captain Courageous*.

On New Gower Street was the Majestic Theatre, commonly called the Bug House, with good reason. There were no toilets in the Bug House, but not to worry! When being admitted the ticket taker, sometimes Clar Wheeler, would tear your admission ticket in half and return you one portion. If nature called you were free to leave the theatre and urinate in any of the laneways nearby. A particularly popular place for the boys was the laneway adjacent to the old City Hall. It wasn't uncommon to see a couple of boys in a pissing contest in that lane to see who could spray the highest. No doubt this practice contributed to the deterioration of that old historic site which in the 1960s was replaced by the present modernistic City Hall, also referred to as Adams Bunker. (It was built under the Mayoralty of Mayor Bill Adams).

If the movie was particularly interesting or compelling the boys wouldn't dare leave, not even to answer nature's call. For that reason, the favourite spot to view a movie at the Majestic was from the balcony. Those in the know would never sit below the balcony on a Saturday afternoon. Many boys bragged about being able to reach the centre row from the balcony.

Just up the street from the Bug House was the Star Theatre on Henry Street. The Star had a toilet. Movies and features at the Star one week, would be played the following week at the Bug House.

On Military Road was the Nickel Theatre—the first theatre to open in St. John's. It opened in 1905 and closed down probably in the late 1950s after the introduction of television. Movies at the Nickel one week would be shown at the York the following week. The Nickel was smaller than the York but, like the York, it was considered modern. It had a bathroom. No pissing in the lanes on Military Road. Perhaps this was to appease His Grace the Roman Catholic Archbishop across the street.

Paramount Theatre: One of the finest movie houses in the Province, the Paramount was another popular entertainment spot for downtown children.

Perhaps the finest Theatre ever to grace our fair City was the old Paramount which opened in the 1940s. It was very plush and futuristic looking. The outside was designed after a popular New York theatre and the interior had a vestibule, modern toilets with multiple urinals, and, in the theatre, cushioned seats. The other theatres all had hard wooden seats.

The Capital Theatre on Henry Street was another plush and modern theatre with plush seats, indoor plumbing and a magnificent screen and curtain area. Another modern theatre was the Cornwall, which lasted only a few years. The Cornwall Theatre was located on LeMarchant Road and had all the amenities of the Capitol and the Paramount. Although the Paramount was the finest of theatres, the one which holds the fondest memories for me is the old York Theatre.

In those days, comic books were immensely popular among children. Kids after reading their comics would go around the neighbourhood knocking on doors asking other kids to exchange comics for books that had not been read by one or the other. This tradition spilled over into the theatres.

Kids would rush to the theatres a half hour before the movie started so as to have an opportunity to exchange comic books. I remember many occasions at the York participating in that ritual. A kid would take an armful of comics and start from the first row working his way to the last. All over the theatre you could hear the chant, "Got any to change?"

When you found someone with comics to change, the bartering began. One kid would hold the books in one arm and flip them over with the free hand. The other kid would recite a litany of "Seen it, seen it, seen it!" or "Got it, got it, got it!" When his eyes focused on one he had not read he'd shout "Take it!" If there were a series of 'not seens' he would recite another litany of, "Take it, take it, take it."

Then without warning the lights would go out, the curtains would pull open and the movie would start. This would abruptly end the exchange of comics and everyone would scatter for their seats. Sometimes, what was happening in the audience was as entertaining as that on the screen. For example, a character around the city at the time was a newspaper deliverer, Frank Milley. Frank walked with a cane in one hand and his papers under the other arm. His hero was Hopalong Cassidy. When a Hoppy movie was on we always knew Frank would be there. We looked upon Frank's attendance with anticipation because we knew that Frank could not distinguish reality from what was happening on the screen. Of course, as youngsters we couldn't always make that distinction either! But while we would be mesmerized by what was transpiring on screen, Frank would be living it.

Frank would make sure his papers were all sold before a Cassidy movie. Inside the theatre he would choose a seat as close to the screen as possible. When the Cassidy movie started so did the fun. "Watch the fellow behind you, Hoppy!" "Look out, the bastard got a gun!" "Don't trust the slut, Hoppy, she's a two timer!" Frank would roar out the warnings to Hoppy everytime he got in a hot situation. Then when a bar room brawl broke out . . . look out for yourself. You were in danger if seated near Frank. Up would come the cane and Frank would swing it: first to the left, then to the right, all the while shouting "Get the hell out, Hoppy, while the going's good!"

I remember one time Frank tossed the cane at a gun toting screen bandit, only to strike little Anthony Murphy on the head. "Jumpin Jesus," shouted Anthony, "Frank will you go to christ home!" People still recall with amusement the day of Frank's wife's funeral. Frank missed it because he was at the York Theatre to see the conclusion of the serial Captain Marvel.

Movies were cheap by today's standards, but pocket money was not easy to come by. I remember when one of my friends went to his father to ask for ten cents to go to the Crescent Theatre to see the movie *Liberty*. These were tough times and ten cents was not always easy to come by. His father reluctantly agreed and as he passed him the dime said, "Here, go down to the Crescent to see *Liberty*; then come home and see poverty."

There were many ways for children to earn pocket money. Need sparks innovation and imagination in the enterprising individual and it's safe to say children downtown were enterprising.

There were the standard ways of earning pocket money which today are still common. For example, baby sitting, selling newspapers, shovelling snow or going on messages for people. But, then there were others which children today couldn't imagine. I remember being among gangs of children going to Job's Wharf when the sealers arrived from their yearly harvest. We were well prepared for the job at hand. Each child had a knife and several wire hoops, usually made from coat hangers or taken off a bundle of splits.

After the sealers unloaded the pelts they turned a blind eye to our presence, knowing it was an opportunity for us to earn some pocket money. We sifted carefully through each and every seal pelt piled high on the wharf looking for scraps of seal meat missed by the seal skinners. When we found a piece of meat we used our pocket knives to cut it from the pelt and then speared the wire hanger through it. It did not take long for one boy to gather seven to ten rings of seal scraps.

We returned to our neighbourhoods covered with seal blood and stinking from seal oil. Hygiene was the furthest thing from our minds. The spattered blood over our clothing was like an advertisement that we had been working among the sealers. This was a source of pride for young boys who admired the courage and strength of the men who yearly went to the northern ice floes.

It's hard to imagine a housewife today purchasing seal scraps to feed her family from raggedy-arsed urchins reeking of seal odour. However, in those days times were tough and seal meat—even scraps—was universally enjoyed and very cheap. Many housewives welcomed and anticipated the little seal salesmen in their neighbourhoods. We had no trouble finding a market for our scraps which we sold for ten to twenty-five cents a ring.

The ladies baked these scraps in a stew of vegetables and gravy covered with a pastry. Unfortunately for us, this was only a seasonal boom and we had to find other ways to earn money during other seasons.

The existence of wood and coal stoves as the primary

source of heat and cooking presented another golden opportunity for us. People needed wood splits to start the fire and coal to keep it going. We would search neighbourhoods and gardens for wood, then chop it up into splits and load the splits into brin bags. A bag of splits sold for twenty-five cents. The stores sold bundles of splits for ten cents, so a whole bag full was a real bargain. But getting a steady supply was a real challenge. Bouncer Abbott, Dickie Murphy, Jack Murphy and I had better luck at this than our buddies. Most of the homes in the area now occupied by City Hall had clapboard falling off.

We used to go into the back gardens of these homes and pull the clapboards off. We did not consider the unfortunate families inside and the effect this had on the comfort of the dwelling. After gathering as much as we could carry we would bring the load to Jack Murphy's garden for processing. With a hatchet each we chopped the wood into little splits, then we would fill the brin bags. Even before it was bagged, housewives would come to us to place an order. Our fuel supply enterprise probably hastened the deterioration of many old St. John's neighbourhoods.

We had several ways of collecting coal, which we sold door to door. Every home used coal, and wagon loads of coal were constantly criss-crossing the city with their deliveries. Full tons, half tons and quarter ton loads were being delivered to homes to be unloaded. Horses pulling a big load of coal often had trouble getting up over some of the hills in town. On a daily basis we watched such horse carts turn around half way up Flower Hill for this very reason. During the process the coal cart was tossed in all directions, causing lumps of coal to spill out onto the street. We followed behind with brin bags picking up the coal lumps. A full bag of coal fetched one dollar and a bucket sold for fifty cents. Even the

City of St. John's Archives

1/2 ton load of coal on its way to soneone's home in St. John's. When coal was delivered to the higher levels the horse would be given the opportunity to drink at the horse trough by the bus terminal on LeMarchant Road.

use of brin bags presented an opportunity to earn money. Stevey Fowler collected and sold us the bags we needed.

Everyday someone in the neighbourhood had coal delivered. The coal man would back his cart into the sidewalk adjacent to the house receiving the delivery and dumped the load onto the ground. He would then collect his money and leave. It was up to the home owner to shovel the coal and bring it into the house for storage in a coal pound. We used to follow the coal cart and after a delivery was made offer to 'shovel it in' for fifty cents. Usually, two boys shared the task and split the money. One would shovel, the other would carry. If we couldn't get the hobble—as odd jobs were called—we would wait until the coal was shovelled in and those who did the job had left. Armed with a brin bag and shovel we could always scrape up a shovel or two of left over coal. A visit to several such sites would earn us enough pocket money for the weekend movies.

Kids further west living in the Patrick Street and Water Street West area had a good and regular source of coal to sell. Much of the coal used in the City came in by train in an open cart. When the train rocked back and forth as it slowed down to approach the station some of the coal was tossed out, landing alongside the tracks. It was a regular sight to see kids with shovels and brin bags standing near the tracks waiting for the black gold to drop from the train.

On special occasions like St. Patrick's Day, Orangeman's Day, Easter and Regatta Day we could make extra money by selling ribbons to celebrate the occasion. The ribbons with rosettes were pinned onto your clothing and were very easy to sell. It seemed everyone wanted a ribbon to mark the occasion. Each event had its own colours. We would line up outside the door of a Mr. Mike Power on George Street who would, after recording our names and addresses, give us a box each to sell. When we returned with our empty boxes he would calculate our earnings at five cents per ribbon and pay us in nickels and dimes.

Discarded soft drink, rum and beer bottles were another source of profit for us. For this project we made a wooden wagon using old coke boxes with wheels taken from worn out carriages and nailed to the bottom. A long rope was tied to the wagon to enable us to pull the cart along. We went door to door collecting these bottles which we sold for prices ranging from one to three cents each. Soft drink bottles sold for one penny and went up to three cents. Rum bottles fetched three and went up to five cents. Beer bottles went from one penny to three cents as well. We sold our bottles to a Mr. D. Noftall, who had a bottle exchange on Casey Street. He later moved his business to Barron Street.

O.L. Vardy, a former Director of Economic Development for Newfoundland, operated a small bottle exchange and stored his bottles in a garage off Lemarchant Road and adjacent to Caul's Field. Inevitably, the boys playing in the field discovered the garage was a storage house for bottles. Several groups of boys protected by the darkness of night raided this treasure for several nights. One group was led by Beaver Murphy, another by Phil Leonard and Robert Woods and a third group by Tucker (Bill) Crotty. The boys would sneak into the garage and remove several cases of bottles at a time. The next day they would take them to the bottle exchange in a building opposite the Royal Aerated Water Company to sell. Unknown to them, the man they were stealing from was the same man to whom they were selling.

When Vardy realized what was happening he called in the police. It was easy enough for the police to solve the mystery. They determined which kids were selling large numbers of bottles that week. The boys were caught. The younger ones were brought home to their parents after being given a stern lecture by the police. The older boys had a court appearance and received a similar warning and lecture from the Judge. Beaver recalled recently that they had narrowly evaded being sent to Reform School.

They weren't the only ones who were willing to risk a brush with the law. When Woolworth's, the first major five and ten-cent store in Newfoundland, opened on Water Street in the mid-1950s, crowds gathered at the opening. They came not only for the bargains but to view a modern day wonder which had not been seen in the City before . . . the escalator. A crowd actually stood around just watching with amazement as the escalator ferried people up and down. Every now and then someone would emerge from the spectators to try the escalator as though it was some sort of adventure.

Among the crowd on opening day was "Jimmy" (not his real name), a thirteen-year-old boy from my neighbourhood who was the eldest in a family of twelve. Jimmy was street wise, and he wasn't beyond delivering a knuckle sandwich to those who crossed him, even older boys. With so many people crowded inside Woolworth's and the distraction caused by the escalator, Jimmy saw an opportunity of self enrichment. Moirs Pot of Gold chocolates were piled almost to the ceiling near the front door. Jimmy, grabbed a box and stuffed it inside his coat. When he attempted to leave the store he was seized by the collar by a security guard who dragged him screaming obscenities and threats all the way to the manager's office at the rear of the store.

Fortunately for Jimmy, the manager was in a benevolent mood and instead of having him charged with shoplifting arranged for the police to bring Jimmy home and report the incident to his parents. The manager, displaying the confidence and wisdom of Solomon, was content to allow the family to dispense the appropriate justice.

Minutes later the police were at Jimmy's door providing his father with a full report on Jimmy's theft at Woolworth's and what the consequences could have been had the manager not been in a forgiving mood. Jimmy's father thanked the police officers and bade them farewell. As they descended the steps of a high gallery they smiled contently upon hearing the father shout, "Get inside young man, I'll deal with you." Meanwhile, inside the house with the door closed, Jimmy's father upped with his hand and struck Jimmy, sending him sprawling across the kitchen floor. He roared at Jimmy, "What did I tell you about stealing . . . where is one box of chocolates going to go among all of us?"

I recall an encounter with Jimmy which originated at Capsules, a swimming hole about a quarter of a mile past the old Bowring park swimming pool. It was my first swim for the summer and I was wearing a new pair of red swimming trunks purchased just the day before. After swimming I changed in a wooded area near the pool. When I turned to pick up my wet trunks to wrap in my towel they were gone. Bouncer said, "Jimmy took em and ran up the bank." When I looked Jimmy had already gone over the peak of the hill overlooking Capsules and was on his way across the big open field heading towards the bus stop on Bay Bulls road. I grabbed my towel and gave chase followed by Bouncer, Dickie Murphy and Jackie Murphy. Halfway across the field we could see Jimmy in the distance getting onto the yellow bus. He took a seat near a window and shook his fist at us as the bus pulled away.

I was determined to retrieve my trunks even at the risk of fisticuffs with the rowdy Jimmy. We caught the next bus and got off on New Gower Street near Jimmy's house. As we approached the house we got a glimpse of Jimmy looking out an upstairs window. When he saw us approaching he disappeared form the window. We expected to be greeted by him at the door with fists raised and ready to fight. Fortunately, his mother answered the door and I told her what happened. My three friends confirmed my claim. She was very nice and invited me into a hallway where she opened a large box. I never saw so many swimming trunks before. There must have been 30 or 40 pairs, in every imaginable colour. "You're not the first one he's robbed," she commented. "If you can find yours anywhere in this you can have them."

I had no trouble finding my swimming wear. But for the longest while after I had to be cautious when walking near Jimmy's neighbourhood. One would have expected that Jimmy's future would involve reform school or prison. However, Jimmy grew up to become a well known and respected businessman in St. John's.

Jimmy was not the only street smart kid on the block. At

ten years of age Pat had wit and the ability to read human nature that put him a step ahead of the rest of us. This ability came into play when he and a friend named Charlie picked up a wallet filled with money near Walsh's Bakery on Central Street. Pat searched the wallet for identification and determined it was owned by a lady on Monroe Street. Charlie suggested they return the wallet and Pat expressed the hope they would fetch a good reward for their deed.

Charlie and Pat stopped in front of Jim Fardy's store exchanging opinions on how much the reward would be and how they would spend it. Charlie longed for a bottle of Spur, a crinkle and an Adler's chocolate bar. Pat also wanted a Spur but preferred a sinker and a Dutch Creme bar. Off they went to Monroe Street anxious to collect the reward, which they felt certain would be given and return to Fardy's to spend it. When the woman came to her door and learned that her lost wallet had been found she was ecstatic. She opened it and after viewing the wad of bills still inside the wallet she compliment the boys on their honesty and told them to wait, noting, "Such honesty is deserving of a reward." She went back into the house. Charlie smiled at Pat and flashed ten fingers suggesting a reward of ten dollars. Pat, also smiling, flashed ten fingers twice, suggesting he expected twenty dollars.

The uncertainty ended when the lady returned to the front door and gave each of them an orange. She thanked them again then closed her door. The boys were not at all happy. When they got by Walsh's barn Pat tossed his orange over the fence and invited Charlie to join him at Fardy's store for some treats. Charlie, sceptical, asked, "Out of what? Ya can't spend oranges!" Pat put his hand in his pocket and withdrew a twenty dollar bill. "Ya didn't think I gave her *all* the money did ya?"

Perhaps to prevent us from entering a life of crime, the city and the church provided many organizations and boys' clubs. The Catholic Boys' Club on St. Clare's Avenue was popular among many of my friends. Another club, the Mounties Club, was also very popular among boys all over the City. This club was operated by one of the City's service clubs at the RCMP barracks on Kenna's Hill. The area is now occupied by the Chalker Place public housing units. I am not sure how many nights per week the club operated but I remember going regularly on Thursday night and Saturday mornings.

Thursday was especially appealing because it was movie night. Following the movie the workers there dished out hot chocolate and biscuits. The hot chocolate was made in huge camp fire style kettles that are no longer used today. The biscuits were donated by bakeries around the City. The hot chocolate was welcomed on cold winter nights when we had to wait on Portugal Cove Road for the bus to take us home.

Saturday mornings were devoted to sporting activities. One of the activities which appealed to me, for a short while anyway, was boxing. I had two fights in the ring. The first against Jackie (Sarge) Murphy, a friend and neighbour from Flower Hill. I was taller and heavier than Jack. But then, so was everyone else. The difference in size made me confident. I pounded Jack until he had enough, then I confidently pranced around the ring waiting my next opponent. I felt I could lick anyone. Boxing was a breeze.

In the ring stepped Pat Hearn, also a friend and neighbour. Pat had a reputation as a good street fighter, but I wasn't deterred. The referee blew his whistle and the bout started. Before the first round was over I thought I was fighting a whole gang. I was being pounded all over the ring. Murphy was in the corner cheering me on. Little did I know this was his sleveen way to get revenge for his defeat. He was shouting, "Keep in there . . . he's not even touchin' ya . . . he's not touchin ya." When the round ended and I went to my corner Murphy was there encouraging me to go back in and chanting, "He's not even touchin ya."

I went back in, and Pat's offensive was even stronger than before. Murphy was still shouting, "He's not even touchin ya . . he's not touchin ya." Reeling from the beating, I got near where Murphy was stand-

Author Jack Fitzgerald: This picture was taken on the day he made his Confirmation. Red rosettes and arm bands were worn for Confirmation, while white was worn for first Holy Communion.

ing at ringside and shouted to him, "If Pat's not touchin me, ya better keep your eyes on the referee. Someone's pounding the piss outa me!" I lost interest in boxing after that fight. I was happy enough to win one out of two fights.

Another active organization for young Catholics was the Total Abstinence Society. The TA, as it was better known, was established in St. John's on May 16, 1858 and had an influence on city life for the next one hundred years. It was a very cultured organization which involved its members in plays, operettas, public speaking and debates. However, when I joined around 1954 the TA was in its final years.

The TA had a juvenile division which met at the TA Hall on Duckworth Street on Sunday afternoons. Members paid dues of five cents per week. To be admitted one had to swear an oath never to partake of alcoholic beverages. There were frequent talks on the evils of alcohol, but there were also games, movies, summer picnics and fun activities for young people.

I enrolled along with a close friend whom I shall call Spuds. Spuds, slow-moving and slow-thinking, was the butt of frequent jokes and pranks. One that I pulled many times, and always with success, was the magic trick of making an egg disappear. I would convince Spuds that I could make the egg disappear by placing it on his head and pulling his beloved red and gold Holy Cross tassel hat down over it. I would recite a litany of magic words, "Abracadabra, Allah Kazam...," and then I would command the egg to disappear by pounding my hand down hard over the hat and smashing the egg into Spuds head. Although Spuds was dull he was big and powerful for his age. I was always convinced that in a rage he could do some real bodily harm to a fellow, so I didn't stay around for any compliments.

Luckily for me, Spuds had a short memory. A few weeks later he would again agree to participate in another disappearing egg trick. This time I would ask him to place it in his pants pocket. Once again I would recite a litany of magic words and conclude with a hard slap to Spuds pocket smashing the egg into an ugly mess. I always managed to escape the scene before Spuds could get his powerful hands around my neck.

Well, Spuds and I joined the TA the same day. We both took the oath,"...never to take a drink,' as the oldtimers would say. Later that evening Spuds mother came to my house all upset and asked me to go talk to Spuds. She said, "Foolish Spuds, says he took the pledge never to drink and now I can't even get him to drink water." I obliged. I went with her and accepted a cup of hot steeped tea to show Spuds it was not a violation of our oath. However, it was no easy task to convince Spuds that the pledge applied only to alcoholic beverages. With the help of his mother we persuaded a very reluctant Spuds to have a drink of water.

But no matter how many worthwhile clubs and organizations we attended, nothing could beat the fun we made for ourselves—like a trip to the city dump. During the early 1950s the dump was still located in the area off Stamp's Lane and Wishing Well Road area. I recall vividly my first visit to the site. I was awe struck at the tons and tons of garbage and the large area it covered. Two boys on Flower Hill with relatives in that area suggested one day that we go with them for a visit to the dump to look for things of value. They told us many interesting and adventurous stories about their escapades to the dump. It was summer. We were on holidays. We wanted adventure. So off we went . . . to the dump.

At the dump, we were surprised to see Flash Kavanagh, a salesman for Walsh's Bakery, back his wagon into the dump and unload boxes of stale cakes, buns and pies. We had no idea that the bakeries unloaded their stale goods in this way. When Flash left we rushed over and opened the top box, which contained lemon pies. A city worker had seen us and was moving in our direction. We realized we were off limits but we were not about to leave without taking some of our discovered treasure. We each grabbed a pie and ran with the worker in chase. We didn't stop running until we got behind St. Theresa's Church. We examined the pies to see if there was any sign of mould and we decided they were edible. So, we opened the cellophane packages and ate as much of the pie as we could, throwing away what we couldn't eat.

Anthony Murphy suggested we take a short cut home along Mundy Pond, which was much larger in those days than it is today. The short cut involved walking along the side of the pond towards Purity Factories. At one point we had to walk on a narrow edge near Purity which was muddy, slippery and about two feet above the water level. I was moving cautiously over the mud bridge when I slipped and went into the water. The boys pulled me out. My parents were not at all happy when they learned where I had been. The idea of an adventure outing to the city dump never again appealed to me.

Not too many kids had their own bicycles in those days, but that didn't stop us from going on adventurous bicycle rides. Several outlets around the city rented bicycles at ten cents and hour. I recall one operating on the lower part of Carter's Hill and another at Pike's Cycle Store on Springdale Street. There were many more around the city. When we decided to rent a bike we made sure we had a place to go. Rarely would we waste the time just riding it around the neighbourhood streets. Where we went depended on how many hours we could rent it. Sometimes, we would go to Bowring Park, or Twin Falls in Mount Pearl. Other occasions took us to Sugar Loaf or Quidi Vidi Lake.

Sometimes when visiting the stores on Water Street we would stop at the old General Post Office. This was an intriguing old building which opened for business on June 7, 1886. What attracted our attention was the swinging entrance doors and giant pillars at the front of the building. The combination attracted many children who liked to play around the pillars or use the swinging doors. I believe the only other place in the city with similar swinging doors was the old Newfoundland Hotel. The old post office was torn down in 1957 to make way for a new one on the same site.

According to Don Wilson—who at the time was Manager of Argo Construction who demolished the old post office—the historic building was structurally sound when destroyed. Mr. Wilson explained that the old building did not serve the needs of the post office and on that basis it was demolished and replaced with a new structure. Mr. Wilson felt that the destruction of the old GPO would not be tolerated today because of widespread recognition of the value of preserving our culture and heritage.

Although we lost a valuable historic site, at least the six pillars that were part of the old structure were rescued and saved. This came about due to the interest of Premier J.R. Smallwood.

While in the process of planning an approach to levelling the old GPO Mr. Wilson was approached by the Premier and asked if the granite pillars could be saved for him. During the discussion Mr. Wilson told Smallwood of his need for an apartment to bring his wife and children down from Sydney, Nova Scotia. Mr. Wilson expressed a particular interest in obtaining an apartment at Linden Court. He got his apartment and Joey got the historic granite columns. But not all six. Four were delivered to Smallwood and used to construct a front gate area for the Premier's residence at Roache's Line. The remaining two were stored on the Argo Property where they remained for fifteen years. Mayor John Murphy then purchased them and brought them to his property at Smithville Crescent where they remain to this day, although I believe they are not yet erected or displayed on the site.

Another fascinating aspect of the destruction of the old GPO was the problem that confronted Argo Construction in demolishing the building without damaging Lee's Department Store or Parker and Monroe's Shoe Store on the opposite side of the street. Fortunately, Mr. Wilson had considerable expertise in this area. While Mr. Wilson had a job to do, it was not one that he relished. Don Wilson regretted that Government had chosen to destroy this historic and beautiful piece of 19th century structure. When I interviewed him in January, 1996 he recalled, "It was in the middle of June

1957 on a Saturday that I directly instructed the crane opera-
tor with a demo ball on how to demolish the old GPO. It was
the hardest day's work of my life. The reason was the building could have toppled across Water Street into a Boot store
and F.P.I Offices upstairs." Demolition of the building took
about two weeks.

The first city post office opened in 1805 on Water Street. It
was operated by Simon Solomon, from his watchmaker store.
H. Mosdell, a local historian, recorded in 1923 that prior to
1850 the post office had operated from several homes around
the city. In 1846 fire destroyed the Solomon operated post
office on Water Street and the operation was moved to
Garrison Hill (the portion that is now part of Bonaventure
Avenue). It remained in operation until 1850 when it was
moved to the new Market House Building on the site now
occupied by the Court House.

W. Solomon took over from his father in 1840 as postmas-
ter. The post office was later moved from the Market House
to W. Solomon's Shop on Solomon's Lane which was adjacent to the old general post on Water Street, further west than
the lane now called Solomon's Lane.

School Days

When Paddy died he was met at Heaven's Gate by St. Peter. Peter opened the gate and invited Paddy to follow him. Down a long golden paved hallway Paddy followed St. Peter. As they approached a large closed door, Paddy could hear the shouting of "Alleluia! Alleluia!"

St. Peter explained to Paddy, "In that room are the Salvation Army souls."

They walked down the hallway a little farther and Paddy could hear people speaking in tongues he could not understand.

St. Peter explained, "In that room are the Pentecostal souls."

As they approached another large closed door, St. Peter placed his fingers over his lips to caution Paddy to remain silent and the two tiptoed past the door.

St. Peter turned and whispered to Paddy, "We have to remain very quiet in this area. In that room are the Roman Catholic Souls, and they think they are the only ones up here."

Before Vatican Two enlightened Catholic theology, it was a common belief among us Catholics that we were the only ones who could earn entry into heaven.

I attended Holy Cross School in St. John's and was taught

by the Irish Christian Brothers. They were excellent teachers and devoted much of their time after school hours to a variety of activities for the students. We had a brass band which was under the control of Brother Jake Batterton. I recall two conductors: Mr. Peter Stapleton, who directed the Royal Newfoundland Regiment Band, and his successor Gordon Pike, who played several decades with the Church Lads Brigade Band and the Regiment Band.

The Holy Cross band was popular in the 1950s and made many public appearances, including performances at the Royal St. John's Regatta and television shows. The band also led the way on Holy Cross Sports Day when several hundred students in school uniforms marched from Patrick Street to the sports field on Leslie Street. The band also performed at the school's Spring Concert and graduation exercises in December. I played first trumpet with the Holy Cross School Band. It was a wonderful experience: I learned to read music, play an instrument, and got out of many classes to attend practice. Some of the other players in the band included Brian and Tom Healy (owners of Healy's Pharmacy). Brian played saxophone, Tom, solo trumpet. Jack Murphy, CD, Chief Warrant Officer and Band Master with the Royal Newfoundland Regiment, played the clarinet. Herb Stead played first trumpet, Leo Stead, saxophone, Jim Jackman, first trumpet. Damien Ryan, now serving as City Clerk for the City of St. John's, played the cymbals.

My most memorable moment with the band was on Monday, October 9, 1961—the official opening of Memorial University. Bands, cheerleaders, and groups from all over the province and outside gathered in the square at Churchill Park before the ceremonies started. It was probably the biggest parade this Province has ever seen. On a stand erected on Elizabeth Avenue in front of the University were some very famous people. In addition to Premier Joey Smallwood, there were Eleanor Roosevelt, wife of U.S. President Franklin Delano Roosevelt; Patricia Murphy, Newfoundland-born entrepreneur who founded the famous Candelite Chain of fancy restaurants in the United States; Baron Edmund de Rothschild; Lord Roy Thompson; Lord Rothmere and E.J. Pratt.

Over the next decade I became a friend of Premier Smallwood and visited him frequently at his Roache's Line home. Just before he suffered a stroke in the late 1980s he approached me to co-write a book with him on the early settlement of Newfoundland. The proposal was shelved after he became sick but I expect that someday I will take his idea and follow through on it.

Though the ceremonies on October 9, 1961, were colourful, I have another, more tragic reason for remembering the day Memorial University officially opened. On that same day my brother Maurice, then twenty-one years old, was killed in an automobile accident on Topsail Road, near the turn off at Paradise.

The band was not the only extracurricular activity at Holy Cross. The brothers organized yearly performances of plays and operettas. Much work and patience went into preparing students for the operettas: HMS Pinafore, the Pirates of Penzance and others. They also organized the school dancers, rhythm band and school choir. A memorable stage production took place when I was in Grade Four. Brother Kiernan put together a play for our class to perform at the annual spring concert. Slacks Harding was given the role of a corpse. All he had to do was to drop to the floor and play dead for about fifteen minutes while the play went ahead. Other boys playing the role of witnesses and police carried on their discussion while Slacks remained motionless on the floor.

Seated in the front seat area were the traditional honoured guests which included Archbishop Patrick Skinner, Monsignor Murphy, and other clerical and civic leaders. Slacks was convincing as a corpse for about five minutes. The audience was unexpectedly distracted when the corpse got a bad case of the hiccups. A very serious murder play suddenly became a comedy. The loudest laughter came from the Archbishop.

Holy Cross also played a major role in the City's sporting life. Some of the finest basketball and soccer teams of the decade were Holy Cross teams. Although I was never a member of any of our school sporting teams, I was an avid supporter and attended our soccer, basketball and hockey games. Many of my classmates played with the school teams and the rest of us were there to lend moral support and encouragement. Not that I didn't think about or want to be on a school team: I did. I even tried out once for the Holy Cross High School Soccer team.

The tryout was held at Eagan Field off Leslie Street, which was our school field. Brother Harry French was coach, and the cream of the crop of the school's athletes were there. My courage and confidence in seeking a spot on the team came from my experience playing neighbourhood soccer with my friends. Some of these included Andy Churchill, Billy Smith, Gus Neville, Dave Squires, Jim Kavanagh, Flush Cooper, and Eric Penney, all of whom were top players. I had some brief success in playing back-yard games with them because of my size—I was much heavier than any of them. When confronted by a player moving the ball towards me I found it effective to meet him head on in sort of a soccer chicken game. If you wanted to get past me you had to meet me head on.

This practice served me well in the back-yards of

Charlton Street. I was certain it would be just as effective in high school soccer. Brother French organized a scrap game to weed out the top players. About ten minutes into the game I found myself facing Peter Byrne who was coming towards me all out and faster than light. Byrne was the school's top athlete. He excelled in soccer, baseball and hockey. He was over six feet tall and built like a solid brick wall. His size, speed and reputation at that point did not deter me. After all, I had sent Gus Neville and Flush Cooper reeling more than once.

Instead of waiting for Byrne to manoeuvre past me I choose to meet him head on. I fixed my sights on him and started to run directly towards him. Closer and closer we came. I increased my speed fully prepared for a collision if necessary, but expecting Byrne would chicken out. He didn't.

When I came to, Brother French was standing over me, asking, "How many fingers am I holding up?" I was lying on a stretcher in the dressing room. I never again showed any interest in playing soccer, either with the school or in the backyards of Charlton Street.

In spite of that, I still enjoyed watching and supporting our school teams in games like the unforgettable high school hockey game at Memorial Stadium between Holy Cross and St. Pat's. Dinty Hearn, the back-up goalie for Holy Cross, inspired humour and fun everywhere he went. Sometimes it was unintentional. During the days leading up to the game Dinty had developed several boils on the back of his neck and it was doubtful that he would be able to play. But when Chowder Finlay, the goalie, failed to turn up, the pressure was on Dint to take to the ice.

He chose to play and when he skated onto the ice the Holy Cross fans came to their feet with whistles and hoots to show their support. However, just minutes into the first period a play took place that is etched in the memory of every

41

fan who attended that day's game, and just about every Holy Cross student has heard about it over the years.

A St. Pat's player got a breakaway and was moving towards the Holy Cross net. Fans on both sides of the Stadium came to their feet; each side cheering their own players. When the player evaded the Holy Cross defence and was getting ready for a shot on goal, Dinty moved a little out of the net, crouched and got ready to stop the assault. The player took a strong, hard slapshot that was heading straight for the net and the first goal of the game.

Dinty's right hand extended to the side like lightning and you could see his whole arm shift backwards as he successfully caught the flying puck in his glove. Holy Cross fans went wild. His fellow players rushed down the ice to congratulate him. Dinty never missed an opportunity to ham it up. He turned to the Holy Cross fans and threw his hands outward and to the side to savour the moment.

In throwing his hands the puck came loose from his glove and went directly into the net. The red light flashed on signalling a goal had been scored. For a moment there was silence in the stadium. Players and fans on both sides seemed stunned by the incident. Then St. Pat's fans went wild, while the mood on the Holy Cross side was suddenly subdued. The heckling from the St. Pat's fans threw Dinty off for the rest of the game which ended in a score of thirteen to one.

One of the players there that day said, "In later years we often kidded Dinty about that game. We used to tell him that St. Pat's scored so many goals on him that the flashing red goal light behind the net burnt the boils off his neck." Lonz Leonard often chided Dinty by telling him that the light flashed on so often because of the goals scored against him that they had to change the bulb several times.

The Christian Brothers were not only active in organizing

sports and performing arts activites; many of them stand out in my memory for their excellence in teaching and helping students. They include Brother Joe Kiernan, Brother Harry French, Brother Gabriel McHugh, Brother Eugene Condon and Brother F. Brennan. Lay teachers whom I recall with esteem and respect include Richard Brodrick, Dan Leonard and Mike McCarthy.

My favourite was Brother Joe Kiernan. He had the most pleasant personality of any person I have ever met. I don't recall ever seeing him angry. He had the rare ability of being able to motivate even the most troublesome boys in school to participate in and enjoy our classroom sessions. He always had an interesting or amusing story to tell before class. I recall on one occasion he brought in a record player with some of the popular songs from New York that year. One of these was "Mr. Tap Toe." He put the record on then gave a demonstration of tap dancing for the class that would be the envy of Fred Astair. Once he had the interest of the entire class he would proceed with his teaching for the day. Brother Kiernan never presided over a boring class.

Sectarianism was still very strong in the 1950s, though the old-time religious bitterness was beginning to diminish. Each religion had its own schools. As children we lived together in neighbourhoods with children of all religions but we were divided in attending school, and in the area of sports.

This division was dramatically evident at hockey games. I remember attending one of the famous Boyle Trophy play-off games at Memorial Stadium. The Guards were challenging St. Bon's who had won the trophy for more than twenty years. Interest in hockey was never higher. And you could tell a person's religion simply by noting on which side of the stadium he was seated. The Catholics predominantly cheered on St. Bon's while the non-Catholics took seats on the opposite side of the stadium to cheer on the Guards. The same practice accompanied basketball, soccer and baseball.

Two holidays during the year increased consciousness of our religious differences: St. Patrick's Day, celebrated by the Irish Catholics, and Orangeman's Day, celebrated by English Protestants. A saying I heard often to describe a calm, quiet situation was,"It's quieter than the Orangemen's Hall on St. Patrick's Day." We sometimes taunted our Protestant friends on Orangeman's Day with an old Irish verse:

> Up the long ladder
> Down the short rope
> To Hell with King Billy
> God bless the pope.
> If that doesn't do
> we'll tear him in two
> and send him to hell
> In his red, white and blue.

But our friendly confrontations left no scars and at the end of the day we would all be together playing box ball or head-on-the roost. We liked and enjoyed our protestant friends though we were often cautious and suspicious of them. However, the differences really had no negative affects on our every day relationships, and I have some splendid memories of all my childhood associations. My Flower Hill neighbourhood was predominantly Catholic. I believe the only non-Catholics among our friends were George and Billy Winsor. Our differences in religion surfaced only when attending organized sporting events. However, when I moved to Charlton Street religious lines were more evenly split. This, however, was not a barrier to friendships. Some of my fondest memories include non-Catholic friends; the Churchills, the Squires, the Penneys, the Smiths, the Janes, the Cooks, the Greenlands.

The awareness that one was attending a denominational school was probably greater in Catholic schools than in non-Catholic schools, due to the presence of brothers and nuns. During the 1950s there were very few lay teachers in the Catholic system. Consequently, even visitors to a Catholic school would notice the difference. The brothers wore the white collar and a long black cassock. The nuns were graced in a black outfit that covered their entire body leaving visible only their face and hands.

There was a daily religious class. Often it was in the religious study classes that we were warned of the moral dangers of associating with Protestants. The teacher would point out that we as Catholics knew the truth regarding our salvation and once knowing the truth could not turn our back on it without risking the loss of our eternal souls. The danger in associating with non-Catholics was that we could develop relationships that could lead to marriage. Mixed marriages presented serious moral problems for the Catholic: In what church would the marriage take place? In what religion would the children be baptized? If we chose any other course but a Catholic marriage and baptism we would be excommunicated from the church and lose our chance of heaven.

But not all our religious instruction was devoted to teaching us to avoid non-Catholics; we also learned about our own Catholic heritage. For example, every Catholic child was familiar with the story of the apparition of Our Lady at Fatima to three small children. A mysterious part of that story which caused much speculation the world over, especially in the late 1950s, was the unopened message Our Lady passed on through the children to the Pope. The message was to be held by the Pope and not to be opened until 1960.

One day in 1957 just prior to the start of our Religious study class at Holy Cross I told Gus Neville and some of the other boys in my class that I knew what was in the message. Before I had a chance to tell them Brother Harry French came in and class began. Gus beckoned to me to write it down, which I did. I passed it to Gus who opened it, grinned, and passed it on. It quickly went through the entire class. Some of the boys smiled, some giggled, some laughed out loud. It caused enough distraction for Brother French to interrupt the class and investigate the source of his competition for class attention.

He saw the note change hands from Larry Mooney to Jim Kavanagh and seized it from Kavanagh's hands. Brother French read the letter and a controlled smile appeared briefly on his face. The note read, "The envelope the Pope has from Our Blessed Lady which he will open in 1960 contains . . . a bill for the Last Supper."

Brother French turned to the class and asked "Who wrote this?" Nobody responded. He asked again, "Who wrote this?" This time Gus Neville put his hand up. Brother French asked, "Gus, do you know who wrote this?"

Gus replied, "You mean the letter from Fatima?"

"Yes," answered Brother French, "Who wrote it?"

Gus stood up and said, "Bro, everyone knows the letter from Fatima was written by the Blessed Virgin."

Brother French threw his hands up in the air and after commenting, "Why do I bother?" went on with the class.

School always started with prayers; students would stand for prayers and be seated afterwards. When the class ended and a new one started prayers were said again. At noon everyday we would say the Angelus. As a matter of fact there was a popular radio program of that era called the

Sacred Heart Hour, part of which was the daily Angelus at 12 noon.

At the end of the day we said the Litany of the Saints. By the time the Litany was started the kids would be anxious to get out of the classroom. You could always detect the restlessness among students at this time of day. The Brother would say an opening prayer and then conclude with the Litany. He would read out from a prayer book a list of Saints' names one at a time. After each name the class would respond "Pray for us." He would recite, "St. John the Baptist," and the class would respond, "Pray for us." He would continue down the list of several pages of saints, and each time the Saint's name was read the students would answer, "Pray for us," until the litany was completed.

I remember on one occasion the Brother teaching our class was called to the principal's office for a meeting just as we were preparing to start the Litany. He invited one of the students, Dinty Hearn, to lead the Litany of the Saints and opened the prayer book to the Litany section. With the Brother gone and the classroom door closed, Dinty requested that we all stand. He then proceeded with the Litany 'Dinty's style.'

"All the saints on page one."

We responded, "Pray for Us."

"All the saints on Page two," Dinty said as he flipped the page.

"Pray for us," we responded. And Dinty went through the several pages of the Litany in this way. It was the fastest time the Litany of the Saints was ever recited in a Catholic School. The next day when the Brother asked if Dinty had covered all the Litany the class responded in unison, "Yes, brother."

Another practice for those of us attending a Catholic

school was the devotion of the first Fridays. This practice required us to go to confession, and attend mass and Holy Communion on the first Friday of each month. On Thursday we were taken class by class from school and marched down the street to St. Patrick's Church where every confessional box was manned by a confessor to accommodate the many students. The girls from St. Patrick's convent were brought to the church at the same time as the boys. However, girls and boys were required to sit on opposite sides of the church. The boys were seated right of centre aisle and the girls seated on the left side. Boys and girls were also divided the same way at Sunday mass. There was a special mass for children each Sunday at 9 am.

On first Fridays we were allowed to come in late for school. This was a concession to enable us to return home for breakfast after receiving Holy Communion. Unlike today, one could not receive Communion without fasting from midnight the night before.

Weekly confessions were held at Catholic Churches everywhere. Confessions at St.Patrick's started at 5 pm. and attracted crowds. Hard wooden benches were arranged on each side of the confessional and people would slide from one spot to the next as the one next in

First Holy Communion was an important day for Catholic children. This photo shows Betty Murphy (Mrs. Andy Churchill) in her first Holy Communion dress.

line at the confession box got up to go into the box.

A story that was often told in our neighbourhood involved a pious old lady named Kitty from Flower Hill and a neighbourhood rogue named Ben. The old lady spent hours in church every day praying and never missed a Saturday confession. On this particular occasion she was sitting next to the box and next in line to go in after Ben. It was common to see people in this position resting against the side of the confession box sometimes with their heads touching the box. Frequently, while in that spot one could hear the conversation coming from inside the box.

On this occasion with the rogue inside the box, the priest got up and left the confessional. Mrs. Cranshaw, who was sitting next to Kitty whispered to her, "Where's the priest gone?"

To which she replied, "If he heard what I'm after hearing he's gone for the police."

During our first year in school we were prepared to receive our first Holy Communion known as the Sacrament of the Eucharist. This involved religious instruction on what Holy Communion was and what was expected of us. The confessional was explained and we were brought to St. Patrick's Church to view the inside of a Confession Box.

The day set for receiving Holy Communion was a big day in our lives. The months of instruction and preparation, all the fussing by adults, and the new clothing with the white ribbons and rosettes gave it all of the trappings of a very special occasion. But there was another, perhaps sacreligious, reason we as children eagerly anticipated making our first communion. It was an opportunity to enrich ourselves financially.

The custom was that after the ceremony at Church the children would visit relatives and friends displaying their first communion outfits. For boys these included a suit, or sport coat and dress pants with a white ribbon tied in a bow around one of the arms. A white silk rosette was pinned to the lapel of the coat. For the girls it was a white dress and white veil similar to a wedding gown. Each person visited would offer money as a gift to the children. The more people you visited the more money you pocketed. So, the kids often went beyond their own neighbourhoods collecting. A similar practice surrounded Confirmation at a later age.

The story of one young girl's first communion illustrates the difficult times that existed in those days. The girl lived with her mother and brother on a street near my home on Flower Hill. After making her first communion she made the traditional call on neighbours in her special outfit and collected several dollars, which was a lot of money in that era. A dollar could purchase ten bars or a dozen Pepsi or enable you to attend the weekly movies at theatres around the City for the next ten weeks.

This little girl had developed by the age of six special qualities of unselfishness and compassion. While the many possibilities for spending money flashed through her mind, she thought of her family. It was a struggle for many families to get by from week to week. She sensed her mother was experiencing a difficult time that week. On her way home she stopped at Fardy's Store to spend some of her money. She glanced over the array of chocolate bars on display in the front window and the trays and jars of candy that lined the counter inside. The poster signs displaying a melting vanilla ice cream or a refreshing bottle of Orange Crush were especially appealing.

The little girl stepped up to the counter and ordered a gallon of potatoes, bologna and a loaf of bread. Instead of succumbing to the temptations that face all children with money in a candy store she chose to make a personal sacrifice to help her family.

Considering the times, I expect there were many other instances of such considerateness and benevolence.

The tradition of attending Lenten Missions was very strong in the 1950s. Each parish had a mission for men, one for women and one for the children. These would generally start on Wednesday night and end on Sunday. They were conducted by missionary fathers who visited from outside the province for that purpose only.

I recall that these were very interesting and lively sessions. The Fathers were always excellent speakers and full of fire and brimstone. A frequent technique of the priest conducting the mission was to stand in the pulpit, make a brief statement and allow ten or fifteen seconds for it to sink in with his audience.

During one such mission Jim Fardy and Jack Kidney were sitting next to each other in church. Both Jim and Jack were respected, well-informed men, who were also the neighbourhood philosophers.

When the church was filled to capacity, which was the case at mission time, the priest ascended the pulpit. He briefly looked over the gathering as though counting people, then raised his hands and in a loud clear voice quoted from the Bible, "In a little while you shall see me. Then in a little while you shall not see me." He then fell out of the pulpit. Fardy turned to Kidney and commented, "Prophetic fellow. Prophetic fellow."

Once a year high school students had a retreat week. During this week there were no regular classes. Students attended school and during the Retreat were not allowed to speak. Guest speakers were lined up to talk about various aspects of religious vocations. An ample supply of religious reading was available in all the classrooms, and a chapel was set up at the Gym. Students were not required to remain in their own classrooms. They could move to other classrooms to inspect the religious displays and literature or go to the chapel. Emphasis was placed on religious vocations so there were pamphlets on the many religious orders. This was a time for meditation and religious enlightenment. Surprisingly, retreats were popular among students.

During one of these yearly retreats, Dinty Hearn managed to pull off a practical joke on the Mother Superior of one of the Convents in St. John's. Earlier in the week one of the boys in class brought in several imported chocolate bars with some natural ingredients. However, in small print on the wrapper was a warning that eating the bar would contribute to flatulence.

The Mother Superior came to our retreat to talk about the lives of several saints who had founded convents and religious orders. When she completed her address she mingled with the students, chatting about her comments among other things. Dinty had one bar left which nobody wanted, for obvious reasons. He politely offered the chocolate to the Mother Superior who graciously accepted and expressed her gratitude to Dinty for his thoughtfulness. To his surprise she opened the bar without reading the warning and consumed it right there in the auditorium. That afternoon while she was addressing other students she cut short her speech, apologized to the student body and excused herself. At this point she was showing some discomfort. She left the hall and we did not see her again.

For the rest of the school year Jim Casey taunted Dinty by telling him the Mother Superior was on her way up over the stairs looking for him.

Retreats were often held during Lent. This was a period

of forty days leading up to Good Friday and Easter Sunday. Lent required personal sacrifices. Everyone gave up something they liked for Lent or took on a special task that would be considered a sacrifice, much like making New Year's resolutions. The challenge was to keep the commitment until Lent ended.

I recall a service in Lent called the cracking of the bones which was held on Holy Thursday. At least, we called it "the cracking of the bones"—I never heard any of our religious education teachers refer to it by this name. It was a solemn occasion held to remember the suffering of Christ and the breaking of his bones on the cross. At this service the lights in church would go off for a minute or so and we would hear the sound of clackers from the front area of the church. At the sound of the clackers we would bow our heads and with our right hand beat our chests three times. This presented an opportunity for devilment for several of our friends. I remember on one occasion Beaver Murphy responded to every cracking sound from the altar with his pocket cracker. It sounded like an echo. Every time he did it Beaver and his friends giggled. Then the light came on and Monsignor Murphy was standing beside him. He had tracked the noise. He grabbed Beaver by the shoulders and evicted him from the church service.

Catholic schools encouraged special devotions to Our Lady and the Sacred Heart of Jesus. A month in each year was dedicated to the devotion of both of them. May was the month of Our Lady while June honoured the Sacred Heart. Each classroom at Holy Cross took on a class project to build a May altar to honour Our Lady and a June Altar to honour the Sacred Heart. There was a beautiful flower garden adjacent to the Monastery on its south side which had a grotto to Our Lady surrounded by roses. At the start of May each year students would line up at the garden for a special prayer service of dedication to Our Lady. A school was erected on that property in the late 1950s.

In school, committees were formed to raise money to purchase items needed to decorate the altar and students participated in designing and decorating the altars. Classes competed with each other in a competition to determine which had the best altar.

The altars were very attractive and artistic. Some characteristics of the May altar included the blue and white crepe paper; the assortment of candles and blue or white candle holders and, most important, a statue of the Blessed Virgin Mary. The June altars to the Sacred Heart were redesigned to include red and white crepe paper and an assortment of red and white candle holders. A statue of the Sacred Heart adorned the top of each altar. Many Catholic homes also followed the practice of having May and June altars.

I recall participating in building a May altar at school during my last year of high school. We had all the materials and candles needed but we did not have a statue of Our Lady. Brother Gabriel McHugh, our teacher, appointed Dinty Hearn and me to go down to the new school on Alexander Street and check around for a statue of Our Lady which was not being used. He suggested several storage areas we should search. We followed his instructions but could not find a statue. After all, every classroom in both schools were involved in building May altars and there was a limited number of Our Lady statues available. Dinty, however was determined not to return to Brother McHugh without a statue.

When we entered the school we noticed that the classrooms were all empty. The teachers at mid-morning would line up all the students and bring them to the bathroom to

Pat Hearn and Mike 'Dinty' Hearn

give them an opportunity to use the facilities. These bath-room breaks were followed by a recess period. Dinty and I strolled from classroom to classroom admiring the variety of May Altar displays. One particular one stood out over the others because of the large statue it featured of Our Lady. The statue was much larger than the others and it was either new or freshly painted. Dinty looked up and down the deserted hallways and suggested this was the ideal statue for our classroom. I protested and argued we would never get it out of the school without being caught. Dinty insisted, "Our Lady is taking a little trip with us," and ordered me to grab one end of the statue. I reluctantly went along with the caper. We managed to get down the hallway, over the stairs and out of the building without being caught. From there we carried it past the Monastery and into Holy Cross on Patrick Street. We got it safely to our classroom on the second floor of the building. Brother McHugh and our fellow students were delighted and complimented us on our effort. Our May altar

Jack Fitzgerald: Picture taken at Holy Cross School the same year he and Dinty swiped a large statue of Our Lady from the school on Alexander Street and placed it in their classroom at Holy Cross on Patrick Street.

that year was magnificent. I was nervous throughout the entire month of May and I expected at any moment Brother McHugh would discover how we got the splendid statue. But to our surprise it was never mentioned. We did however hear from our friends at the other school about one of the Brothers there being upset over the disappearance of his statue. Only Dinty and I knew the disappearance was certainly no miracle.

Dinty was popular among the students from the day he started school. He was independent minded and fearless in expressing his opinion. During his first week in school he clashed with Brother T. I. Murphy. The incident was sparked when Dinty got up from his desk and left the classroom. He came back ten minutes later and took his seat. Brother Murphy ordered him to stand up and asked him where he had gone. Dinty said he had to go to the bathroom. Brother Murphy was angered by the response and warned Dinty that he couldn't go to the bathroom without asking. He told Dinty, "If you got to use the toilet, put your hand up." Dinty responded, "How's that going to stop it?"

Throughout my school years I was rarely a problem for teachers. Generally, I respected my teachers and paid attention in class. But that is not to say there were not moments when I displayed a bit of devilment or participated in pranks perpetrated by others.

Once during a Geography class I contributed to a clash between the teacher and a student that resulted in the student being disciplined. The teacher was Mr. Richard Brodrick, who was a very good teacher and liked by the students. I shared a double desk and seat with Flush Cooper who was also a neighbour of mine. During this particular class Flush was not paying attention. He and Gus Neville were flicking papers back and forth whenever Mr. Brodrick turned away from the class to work on the blackboard.

The topic of discussion was the minerals of Newfoundland. I noticed on several occasions that Mr. Brodrick had cast his eye towards Flush and Gus and I expected the boom to be lowered at any minute.

Instead, Mr. Brodrick asked a question: "What are the two main minerals of Newfoundland?" Anyone paying attention could have easily answered the question correctly. Mr. Brodrick glanced towards Flush who was sliding back into the seat from making a smack at Gus. "You answer my question, Flush!" he ordered. But he did not repeat the question, and Flush obviously had not heard it. I was sitting next to him, resting my head on my hand with my elbow resting on the desk and my hand partly covering my mouth. I was facing Flush and Mr. Brodrick could not see my face from where he stood. Flush looked towards me, expecting me to bail him out. I didn't disappoint him. "Fish and Caribou," I whispered.

"Fish and Caribou," Flush confidently shouted. The class broke-up with laughter. Mr. Brodrick, outraged by the answer retorted, "Since when did fish and caribou become minerals?!" He ordered Flush to stand on the desk so all students could see him and he berated him for not paying attention. For added punishment, Flush was kept in for an hour after school and had to write 100 times, "I must pay attention in class." For the rest of that week I did my best to avoid contact with Gus and Flush after school. As a matter of fact I did a lot of running that week with Gus and Flush close behind.

Another amusing incident involved Brother G. Moore, whom students called "Butsy"— but only behind his back. Brother Moore was a colourful and effective teacher. He was about 5'6" tall and overweight with a round cherubic face. As a matter of fact, he bore a close resemblance to the great American comedian, Jackie Gleason.

I recall well an incident in one of his French classes which set the class in uproarious laughter. Brother Moore was standing at the front of the class leading us in the declension of the French verb Fini, pronounced Finney. He would pronounce the words and the class in unison would repeat them . . . over and over and over. He did this to drill the verbs into our memory. He would shout, Je Fini, we would respond, "Je Fini"; he would say, "Tu Fini" and we would repeat, "Tu Fini," and the same for Il fini, Elle Fini, and all the rest.

Seated in front of the classroom near where Brother Moore was standing was a student named Jim Finney. Finney was not paying attention to the lesson. He was amusing himself with some elastic bands which he was flicking at other students. Brother Moore caught Finney's actions from the corner of his eye and moved slowly towards him without changing the tone of his voice or the pace of his declensions. He moved closer and closer to Finney still leading the class with; "Je fini, Tu fini, Il Fini . . . Elle Fini." Without warning, and just as Finney was drawing back a rubber band to flick at Winst Noftall, Butsy grabbed him by the shoulders and rushed him out the door shouting, "Goooooooooooo Finney."

With Finney outside the classroom and the boys laughing uncontrollably, Butsy's anger dissipated and he must have realized the humour of the situation. He sat at his desk, head down, hands clasped and joined in the laughter. Brother Moore was a very good teacher and was respected and liked by the student body.

With two students sharing the one desk, cheating on tests was common. All a student had to do was peek over at his partner's test paper and copy directly. However, there were pitfalls for those who used this tactic, as Frank Murphy found out in Grade Five at Holy Cross. He was sharing a seat with Jackie Kavanagh during a Geography test. Frank had not prepared for it and was confounded when he read the test questions. Frank glanced over and saw Jackie writing away on his paper. Frank slid down in his seat and, glancing at Jackie's test paper, began to copy the answers. In his eagerness to get as much information as possible he copied down everything on Jackie's paper—including Jackie's name. When Br. T.I. Murphy corrected the papers the next day he noted he had two test papers from Jackie Kavanagh and none from Frank Murphy. It didn't take him long to solve the mystery. Frank was given a big zero in the test and had to stay in after school every day for two weeks.

We did not need an alarm clock to get up for school in the mornings. The CN Dockyard had a time whistle that shrilled throughout the West End at designated times during the day. It went off at the 8 am, starting time of the work day. This was also the signal for most kids to get up for school, which started at 9 am. The noon day whistle signalled the lunch break for the workers. But for the students and Catholics of the West End it was also the time for the daily Angelus. People set their clocks by these whistles. Of course, there was also the noon day gun from Signal Hill which was heard all over the City.

The structure of neighbourhoods was very different from the modern day neighbourhood. Every neighbourhood was like a little village. Each had a confectionery store, grocery store, chinese laundry, meat market, barber shop and shoemaker shop. The shoemaker shop today is as extinct as the chinese laundry and meat market, but in those days we were dependent on them. People had their shoes repaired several times before replacing them with new ones. In my neighbourhood there were two shoemaker shops: Williams on Flower Hill and Jack Kidney's on Brazil Square.

I recall waiting in Williams' Shoemaker Shop at 8:15 am on a school day while Mr. Williams skillfully put new soles and heels on my shoes so I could wear them to school. A new pair of John Whites at Parker and Monroe's sold for less than ten dollars, a princely sum in those days. The shoemaker however, could put soles and heels on a worn out pair of shoes for about two dollars. The shoemaker also made leather book bags to carry our books to and from school. These were necessary especially in winter months and bad weather. Book bags were given as birthday and Christmas gifts and were very welcomed. Jack Kidney and Mr. Williams made some excellent school bags. It was said that when an autopsy was performed on an oldtimer named George who had not washed or changed clothes for most of his life they found a bookbag on his back made by Kidney.

Kidney had an old pot-bellied stove in his store and during winter months neighbourhood oldtimers would sit around it drinking tea and debating the great political issues of the day. Jack was well read and knowledgable on current affairs. Some of the best and liveliest discussions took place between Kidney and Jim Fardy. Jim was also well read and knowledgeable on current events. He had an analytical mind and was well respected in our neighbourhood.

Politicians who knew the centre town well would always seek out the council of Kidney and Fardy. Sometimes Kidney would become so embroiled in the hot stove debates in the back of his store that he would lose track of a pair of shoes. The kids in the neighbourhood knew this. One day on the way home from school with Dickie Murphy we stopped at Kidney's to pick up Dickie's shoes. Dickie told me he really didn't have any shoes in for repair but he would get a pair from Jack. Dickie said, "The time is ripe. Jack got a crowd in back today." Whenever Jack was holding council and couldn't find a pair of shoes quickly he would suggest you go pick out a pair from among the ones on his shelves, since he had shelves of shoes with repairs finished and waiting to be picked up.

We entered the store. The little bell on the door tingled and Jack soon appeared from the back room, looking very much like a shoemaker in a fairy tale. He wore a leather apron, had his long white hair tossed back over his head and wore his spectacles down over his nose. Dickie asked, "I'm here to pick up me shoes. Richard Murhpy's the name." Jack began searching shelf after shelf for the shoes. Occasionally, he would turn to Dickie to ask for a description of the shoes, "What size are they?" or What colour are they?" or "When did you bring them in?"

Finally in desperation and anxious to get back to the hot stove debate, Jack threw his arms in the air and said, "The only thing I can see, is that I must have given them to someone else. Go into the back of the store and see if you can find a pair like them." Dickie went in and a few minutes later came out with a pair just like new and his right size. He had no idea who really owned them. We laughed all the way home.

We were enjoying Dickie's success so much we hardly noticed Rick Harris going into the store as we left. Rick, who was the son of the famous New Gower Street Barber, had one leg shorter than the other. Whenever he bought new shoes, Kidney always put a lift on one of the shoes.

It didn't take Dickie long to discover whose shoes he had taken, nor did it take a Sherlock Holmes to solve the case of Rick Harris's missing shoes. Dickie looked really odd limping to school the next day to compensate for one shoe being higher than the other.

There were several barber shops in my neighbourhood but Harris' on Water Street west of the Belmont was my favourite. Like Kidney's and Fardy's the Harris barber shop was a fascinating place to visit. Children were amazed at the stuffed owl on display in the shop window. The owl was later stolen and never retrieved. But that was not the only attraction. Harris had the reputation of being the City's finest chess player and everyone wanted to play him. Even to play and lose against Harris was something to boast about. There was always a game of chess going on in the shop and Harris had such a grasp of the game that he could cut hair and still follow his game attentively.

When Abbass's Barber Shop opened directly across the street from Harris's, rivalry instantly developed. Many small stores along New Gower Street put wooden shutters over their windows when closing at night. If you saw a shop owner bringing out his shutters you knew it was closing time.

Harris often irritated old Abbass by bringing out his shutters and putting them in place long before regular closing hours. Shutters were held in place by bolts which took awhile to tighten. Mr. Harris pretended to be bolting his

L-R: R. (Dick) Harris, Mr. Wadden, Pat Hunt, Mr. Murphy and Roy Barnes

windows and always aware that Abbass was watching from his shop window. Abbass wouldn't dare close his shop before Harris because of the possibility of losing a customer.

When Harris went into his store and switched out the lights—out would come Abbass with his shutters. Mr. Harris would watch through a darkened hall window until Abbass had finished bolting his windows. Then he would turn his lights on and remove his shutters—which was easy to do, since they had not been bolted.

The price of haircuts was another source of friction between the two adversaries. Haircuts were twenty five cents. Abbass dropped his to fifteen cents and Harris began losing customers. However, the customers would turn up at Harris's several days later pleading with him to fix the cut Abbass had given them. This practice became so common that in response to the Abbass window sign "Hair cuts 15 cents,"Harris placed a sign stating, "We repair 15 cent haircuts."

Every neighbourhood had a fire alarm box erected on a

light pole about five feet from the ground. In case of fire, people would rush to the alarm box and pull down a lever which would cause the alarm to ring at one of the City's several fire department's. This was necessary because phones were still a luxury in the City and those who did have one were on a party line with three other families. It was not always easy getting a line when you wanted one.

I remember well, the fire alarm box on the pole in front of the Brownsdale Hotel at the corner of New Gower Street and Brazil Square. The pole there was unlike the other poles in our area. It was a steel structure which looked like a ladder, and had steel rungs which enabled a person to easily climb it.

One day I was walking home from school with Bouncer Abbott, Billy Abbott, Dave Roache, Jack Murphy, Charlie Fowler and George Gillett. Bouncer had a flair for finding adventure and excitement and if such situations were not available he would instigate one. On this occasion he did just that.

As we approached the pole with the fire alarm box, Bouncer told the younger boys that the box on the pole contained candy. All they had to do was climb up, and pull on the little lever and candy would flow out. Billy and Dave were a little younger than the rest of us and they believed Bouncer's claim that candy could easily be extracted from the box.

Billy gave Dave his book bag to hold on and he climbed up the several rungs until he could reach the little box. By the time he extended his arm to pull the lever the rest of us were half way up Brazil Square. We didn't stop running until we got home.

Several minutes later the air was filled with the sound of clanging bells and sirens as fire cars sped to answer the alarm. We heard the noise but could only wonder as to what was

Corner of Flower Hill and Central Street.

happening at the alarm box. Our curiosity soon ended. I could hear the siren getting closer and closer. It sounded like it was right in front of our kitchen door. We lived next door to the Abbotts. I went out to look and there was the bright red fire engine, with several firemen hanging on the sides and back and Billy sitting in the front seat with the driver. I wasn't the only person to come outside to see the fire truck. Every neighbour on the hill came out thinking there was a fire in the area.

Billy was crying. He knew he was in trouble and believed it was not his fault. The fire chief took him by the arm and brought him to his front door. Luckily for Billy, his father was not home. His mother Alice answered the door and the fireman passed Billy over to her with a complaint that he had rung in a false fire alarm. The chief lectured Billy on the consequences of ringing in false alarms and warned him that if he ever did it again he would be brought to the police station instead of home.

Meanwhile, Dave Roache escaped getting in trouble. He had waited around with Billy hoping for candy, but realized they were in trouble when the fire trucks began pulling in alongside them. Dave denied over and over again to the firemen that he had anything to do with sending the false alarm. He even claimed he didn't know Billy. The firemen believed him and allowed him to go home on his own. It was weeks before Billy spoke to Dave after the incident and months before he ever walked home again in the company of Bouncer.

Idle Mind—Devil's Workshop

In addition to the games that amused us as children, many novelty songs caught our imagination. I don't remember the correct names of all of them, but we loved songs like, 'Get outa here with your boom, boom, boom', 'Open the Door Richard', 'I got a Lovely Bunch of Coco Nuts,' 'Doggie in the Window', 'Ma Gave Me a Nickel', and 'If You Don't Want My Peaches, Get Outa My Tree.' When we tired of playing games, we would sit on someone's doorstep and sing these songs. A popular spot for doing this was on the steps of Edney's Store opposite Walsh's Bakery on Central Street, or Mike Murphy's steps at the corner of Flower Hill and Central.

Ma Gave me A Nickel was the song that we used to exact revenge on one of the older boys in the neighbourhood who often took over our games and bullied us. Stan Dooley was several years older than any of the boys in our group and he enjoyed being able to lord over us. No matter what game we chose to play, Stan, because of his age and size, had the advantage over us. We didn't have a chance in head on the roost, hoist your sails, boggers or any of the games we played. When the games ended and we were dead tired we would sit on the steps and sing songs. Immediately, Stan was up on his feet with his arms waving like Arthur Fiedler directing the Boston Pops and singing at the top of his lungs. You could tell by the defiant look on his face that he enjoyed being leader.

Well, Stan had a speech impediment. He stuttered frequently. When he stuttered, he closed his eyes, his face straining as he tried to get out the words, and he would slap his right leg with his right hand when the word broke loose. Jackie Murphy or Charlie Fowler would start the song, *Ma gave me a Nickel* . . . and we would all join in. Needless to say Stan would be the loudest.

I don't remember very much of the song, but if you recognize it you are over fifty. In unison we sang,

> Ma gave me a Nickel
> to buy a pickle,
> I didn't buy a pickle
> I bought some chewing gum!

Each verse was followed by a chorus that sounded like someone stuttering and it was here we equalled the score with Stan. The chorus would go . . .

> Some, chew, chew, chew
> chew, chewing gum . . . I love my chewing gum . . .
> etc.

At the end of each verse we would all stop singing and focus our attention on Stan as he sang the chorus. Eyes closed, arms waving, face straining, right hand raised for the inevitable slap on the right leg, lost in the tune and lyrics of the song Stan would stutter out, "Some, chew, chew, chew, chew, chewing gum!" We would bite our tongues, hold our hands over our mouths, bow our heads—anything to conceal our delight and amusement over Stan's performance.

After a few performances word got around the neighbourhood. The boys Stan's own age would encourage us to get the sing-along going. However, they made no attempt to conceal their laughter. Stan caught on quickly. He didn't bother us after that and chose to hang out with boys his own age on Monroe Street.

Some years later, Stan's desire to impress the gang and be a leader got one of his best friends into a life threatening situation. At the age of eighteen Stan was anxious to join the army and participate in the Korean War. However, he did not want to join up alone. So, time after time he would encourage the boys hanging out in front of Fardy's store to go with him to the recruiting office. He kept everyone informed on the latest news from the war front and would romanticize about what it would be like to be in the middle of the action. Over and over again he challenged his buddy John (Whitey) Reardigan to go with him to join up. When Whitey refused Stan would call him a coward and insinuate he didn't have the guts to go to war. Three months later Stan was on the corner showing the boys newspaper pictures of Whitey behind a large gun at the Korean Front.

Whitey had succumbed to Stan's taunting and went with him to join the Army. Stan was screened out, Whitey was accepted and after a short stint of training was shipped to the war front. Whitey was not at all happy about the outcome but could do nothing about it. The boys never let Stan forget his failure to make the grade. They used to claim that Stan failed the IQ test. According to the claim, Stan was shown a picture of a teapot with no handle and asked to explain what was wrong with the picture. Stan said, "Nothing's wrong with it. We got one home just like it." When Whitey returned from the Korean War he was the local hero and had lots of hair raising stories to tell. Occasionally, he would walk in on Stan talking about war records and Whitey would interject, "Go way, Stan, the only war record you got is Vera Lynn singing the White Cliffs of Dover." Stan was later accepted into the army. He passed away several years ago and the boys still tell the story about him and Whitey.

Another song we had a lot of fun with was the Shaving Cream Song. I don't know if that was a recorded song, or one made up by Harry Murphy of Flower Hill. At least Harry was the first person I heard singing it and it was quickly picked up around the neighbourhood. Not only did the kids have sing-along's on the steps but on hot summer nights whole families would sit out on their doorsteps. It was not at all unusual for several families to join in singing. The adults liked songs like: "Four Leaf Clover," "If I were a Blackbird," "How Can You buy Kilarney?" and so on. No such sing-along would pass without Harry's shaving cream song.

I recall some of the words:

> A baby fell out of the window
> We thought for sure it would hit . . .
> then suddenly out of nowhere
> it fell in a bucket of shhhhhhhhhaving cream,
> always be clean, shave every day and you'll
> always be clean.

These were the days of the night-soil carts (shit cars). A child's imagination could easily conjure up a picture of a baby falling from a window into one of a parade of night soil buckets that adorned the downtown streets. The song caught our attention and when we sang it we would change the shhhhhaving cream to a bucket of shhhhhhit. Of course we would be admonished by our parents, but being very young kids we would get away with it over and over. Even today I am not so sure that we did not have the right version of Harry's song.

When the family of Harry and Mary Murphy held a reunion at the Star Hall during July 1995 these were among the songs we all remembered and sang with amusement. Harry and Mary would have been proud of the 163 descendants who gathered to honour their memory at a special dinner also held at the Star. I was invited to act as master of ceremonies for the event and I was the only non-family member invited. Several Murphy grand-children sang a medley of Harry and Mary's old time favourites which was well received by the audience which eagerly joined in the sing-a-long.

Another, song we used to taunt a girl who lived in the upper area of Flower Hill was "Dirty Lil." This was sung with a calypso beat:

> Dirty Lil, Dirty Lil,
> Lives on top of Flower Hill,
> Never took a bath
> and never will
> Yuck! Phooey! dirty Lil.

We would sometimes substitute a hawk spit for "Yuck." If you don't know what a hawk spit sounds like, ask any townie. The song was not really a reflection on Lil's hygiene; it was just one of those things boys would do when they could inspire an angry reaction from one of the girls. And boy, did Lil get angry.

Lil had a bad reputation around the neighbourhood. One of the stories told about her involved the time she fell asleep at Caul's Field, a meadow located off Brazil Street and bordered by Monroe Street on the South and LeMarchant Road on the north. Caul's Funeral home grazed and housed their horses in the meadow. As well, the boys from the neighbourhood used the meadow as a ball field.

Lil once fell asleep on a patch of grass near where the boys were playing ball. One of Caul's horses grazing nearby accidently stepped on Lil. The pressure awoke her and she responded instantly with her two hands waving in the air and shouting, "All right boys, one at a time . . . one at a time."

I can't vouch for the authenticity of the story, but it was told so often we believed it. Over a period of time Lil earned a nickname which one dared not mention within striking distance of her. It was a question, rather than a name. But mention the question today to many who grew up in the Flower Hill area and you will get a smile and a name. As young boys we would stand on the corner of Flower Hill and Central Street and when Lil was half way up the Hill, shout, "How's ya belly for biscuits?" Her response was always the same, "How's ya tongue for lickin' them off!" Even today, I am often asked by old friends if "How's ya belly?" is still alive.

Another story told about Lil relates to her being attacked by several American soldiers from Pepperell. Lil was walking her dog one evening near Standard Bedding at the foot of Flower Hill when four soldiers grabbed her with the dog and dragged them into the laneway. Harry Murphy was walking up the hill, on his way home from Chaytor's Butcher Shop on New Gower Street. When Harry saw the incident he ran over to the laneway and shouted to the soldiers, "Hey, do whatever ye want with Lil, but leave that dog alone." Lil was the butt of many jokes and even today the exaggerations regarding her are still popular when people reminisce over the good old days. Lil in later years married an American soldier and moved to the United States. We never heard from her again.

I don't believe people in any other part of the City had as much proclivity for assigning nick-names to people as those who lived in the Flower Hill area. There was Salt Water Bill, Salt Water Oranges, Blue Farts, Motar Wally, Silver Dollar, Argo, and many others. Sometimes, as in the case of "How's ya Belly?" a whole phrase was used as a nick-name. The phrase style nick-name was usually sparked by some quirk of personality or other characteristic of the individual. For example, one lady who lived on Clifford Street had an uppity air about her that offended some people. She often ignored neighbours, passing them by with her head in the air. They used to say, "Her head is so high in the air she can see over the clouds." This meant she was a snob or snotty person. She was nick-named, "How's the weather up there?" While the adults referred to her by this phrase they dared not say it in her majestic presence. However, as kids we heard the adults talk at home, in the stores and so on. Whenever she passed a group of kids on the street one was certain to address her with, "How's the weather up there?"

Another gentlemen had a peculiar walk which was obvious. When he walked he was bent over so that the upper part of his body extended at a forty-five degree angle over his lower body. His arms swung as rapidly as his feet moved. He was nick-named, "Here's me head. Me arse is coming." Another character at the time was a powerful man named Allan. He was a common sight around the downtown streets with his wheelbarrow and was always around to salvage wood when a house was being torn down. He was called, "Allan, Allan, shit a gallon." Motar Wally lived on Casey Street and also pushed a wheelbarrow. He sold brooms, splits and loose coal door to door. Motar had a very good singing voice and loved classical music. The older boys would entice him to lay down his wheelbarrow and sing his favourite classical pieces.

Many of the boys had nick-names. Robert Abbott was Bouncer, Jimmy Murphy was Nanna and is still known as Nanna today. Then there was Fatso (Pat) Ryall who made his mark playing baseball, Lorraine (Muck) Abbott and her sister Betty (Duck) Abbott. Little Da was a name we called one of the boys who emulated the characteristics of his grandfather. Hitler was the name reserved for a man who worked on the coal boats and bore a physical resemblance to Adolph Hitler. Then there was Kip Malone, Cuff Murphy, Donkey Dick McGrath, Spotty Baird, Phil (Lonz) Leonard one of the top baseball players of the 1960s, Doc Butler and Buff O'Keefe. Other names included Gerry 'Niggey' Sears, Frank 'Famy' Sears, Eck 'The Lung' Aylward, Hop and Slop Jackman, Fluke Noftall and Flash Kavanagh.

Pussy-foot was a name we called a woman in the area. In those days there were no private phone lines. We had four people on a line which was called a party line. Pussy was on the same line as Bouncer. Whenever he picked up the phone and recognized her voice he would taunt her by saying "Puss . . . Puss . . . Puss." She learned it was Bouncer who was listening in on her line and reported him to his mother. That put a stop to Puss . . . Puss on the line.

Townies were as adept at using metaphors as they were in innovating unique nick-names. For example, an untidy, unkempt person was described as being like ". . . a Friday shit going to a Saturday market." Another metaphor to describe a mean or stingy person was, "He's so mean, he wouldn't give his shit to the crows." A dull or stupid person was referred to as being, ". . . like Mutt's Dog." Usually enough said. If you asked for an explanation you would be told, "Mutt's dog put his arse in the water to get a drink."

We had another description which applied to any person who had multiple skills and could do almost anything. Jack Churchill who lived on Coronation Street was such a person. He could fix cars, do plumbing, electrical work, carpentry. He was frequently called upon by neighbours to get them out of a jam when confronted with some kind of household calamity like pipes breaking, car trouble and so on. In describing Jack's abilities we would say, "Jack Churchill could put a canvas arse on a cat," which meant he could do anything.

Children usually accept nicknames without questioning any explanation for the name. However, there are exceptions to every rule, and in our neighbourhood there was an exception to this. One of the boys had an explanation for every nickname in the neighbourhood. He was Jerome Gillett, who himself was nicknamed Trapper. His presence in Jim Fardy's store at the same time Donkey Dick McGrath and Kit Martin were present made for a memorable situation.

Kit Martin, was a pious, humble, unpretentious person but naive to the ways of the world. She was as close to a saint as you are going to find in this world. She attended daily mass and communion, weekly confessions and recited the rosary several times a day. She was liked by everyone in the neighbourhood and the women especially welcomed chatting with her because she was a most interesting conversationalist.

Donkey Dick had ordered a couple of slices of bologna and a bottle of Spur. He bade good day to Jim and Kitty and left the store. Once he closed the door behind him, Kitty walked over and peered at him through the window. It was obvious that she was puzzled about something. Jim was placing the bologna back in the fridge when Kit turned towards him and asked, "Jimmy, why do they call that fellow Donkey Dick?"

Jim, a religious person himself and a true gentleman, turned crimson red from the neck up as he tried to come up with a reasonable answer. "I don't really know, the boys up on Cabot Street gave him that name," Jim replied. Trapper Gillett, then about eleven years old, was sitting on a bundle of splits finishing off a Sinker (large cake square). He stood up, brushed the crumbs off and interjected, "Kit, I can tell why they call him Donkey Dick. It's because he got a . . ." Kit was now facing Trapper with her back to Jim. Jim picked up his cutting knife, the one he had used to slice the bologna and facing Trapper simulated a throat cutting movement at the same time and in a very stern voice said, "That's enough Trapper, you better go on home now. Your mother warned you about hanging around." Trapper left the store and Jim quickly changed the subject.

Jim Fardy loved to play jokes on some of his customers, and on another occasion it was poor Kitty Martin again who was his unintended victim. Jim had purchased a Whoopie cushion from Jackie Smith's Novelties on New Gower Street, and he used to place the whoopie cushion under the cushion covering a rocking chair which sat outside his counter for customers. However, many of the boys would use the chair when hanging out in the store having a Pepsi. The cushion had embarrassed many of the boys and Jim felt certain there were still a few who had not heard about it when he placed it that night.

From the backroom of the store Jim heard the ring of the bell which hung over his front door and would jingle whenever anybody entered or left the store. At last someone was coming in and he could have a little fun. It was not, however any of the boys from the neighbourhood. Jim had no time to retrieve the cushion before Kitty Martin planted herself down into the rocking chair with force to demonstrate how tired she had been from walking down from St. Patrick's Church after evening prayers.

A whoopie cushion never worked better before or since. Poor Kitty, terribly embarrassed said in a faint voice to Jim, "Jesus, Mary and Joseph, Jim it must have been the cabbage I had for supper."

Jim Fardy's wonderful wit and sense of humour lasted right up to the time he passed away in December, 1994. When I visited him a week before his death at St. Clare's Hospital, he told me how his foreign-born doctor, who spoke broken English, had told him that he had terminal cancer. Jim asked how long he had left, but the Doctor was reluctant to answer the question. So, Jim said, "I told him I didn't expect to know the exact date, but just wondered if he could give me a ball-park figure . . . then I had to go and explain to him what a ball park was!"

Days before his passing he still lit up those around him with his humour. At age seventy, he had been smoking since he was ten years old. He told me during my last visit with him, "The irony of it. I smoked sixty years, and I end up getting cancer in the bowels." Jim claimed (tongue in cheek) that he never ignored the warnings on cigarette packages. He said when he purchased a package of cigarettes he always asked the clerk not to give him the ones with the warning on the package that they cause cancer. He would add, "I asked for the ones with the warning that cigarette smoking was harmful to babies . . . they were not as bad."

Fardy's store was just one of many popular hang-outs for young people in our neighbourhood in the 1950s. We had no neighbourhood playgrounds as we have today but there were lots of open spaces. Meadows and fields dotted the city landscape and these made excellent play areas for children. In our neighbourhood there was Martin's Meadow which was twice the size it is today. A public housing development on Livingstone Street cut through the meadow and reduced its size. Off Central Street just east of Flower Hill was Cooper's Lane. It got its name from a cooper's shop at the bottom of the lane. However, the laneway led to an open field with a bank on the north side that was especially good for sliding in wintertime. It was also an out of the way place to build bough houses after Christmas when people discarded their trees. That area is now occupied by the office building which is part of the Delta Hotel Complex.

On the western end of Central Street bounded by Walsh's Bakery, Caul's Lane, Casey Street and Sheehan Shute Lane was another open field. Off Brazil Street in the area now occupied by Cabot Apartments was Caul's Field, the field where Lil was so rudely awakened by the horse from Caul's Funeral Home. It was also a popular field for baseball, softball and soccer and we developed great skills in circumventing the horse manure which dotted the field. But occasionally an enthusiastic player would let his guard down and slide into one of the puddles of manure.

Up the street from Caul's Field was the Prince of Wales Field. This was popular for playing ball as well. It was a large field adjacent to the original Prince of Wales College but later occupied by Harrington School. Further west was the Knights of Columbus Field which was an extra large field and is now used by the K of C as a parking lot with another portion occupied by Holy Cross School. This field was the largest in our area.

There were two open fields off New Gower Street near Power's Candy Store. Behind the store adjacent to Horwood Lumber Yard was an area called the Battlefield. Opposite Power's Candy Store on the Southside of New Gower Street was another playing field. Further west was Thompson's

Field which was later converted into a housing subdivision now called Thompson Place. Eagan Field off Leslie Street was owned by Holy Cross and used by the school for their sporting activities. That field today is owned and operated by the City of St. John's.

Many lifelong friendships and romances began in these fields. One such romance was that of Frank (Teeney) Murphy and Jean Baird. Frank lived on Flower Hill and Jean next door to Power's Candy Store. Neighbourhoods organized their own sporting activities, which were not developed organizations as we have today but rather, spontaneous challenges from the boys of one street to those of another.

During a challenge game between the Flower Hill boys and the boys from New Gower Street, Frank met Jean in a peculiar way. While the boys played ball, the girls would sit on a fence to cheer (or jeer) them on, depending on circumstances. Frank was playing centre field near the fence where Jean, her sister Anita (Neat) and several other girls had gathered.

A batter hit the ball past Frank, over the fence and onto the road. Players had only the one ball and the loss of that ball could end the game. Frank jumped the fence to retrieve the ball but the girls beat him to it. The ball ended up in Jean's hand and she ignored the demands from the boys to return it. Instead she ran across the street and up a laneway into the Battlefield behind Power's Store. Jean was followed by her sister, their friends and every boy on the playing field.

When they finally cornered her she tossed the ball over a fence and ran in the opposite direction. Frank went over the fence, got the ball, and the game went ahead. After the game Frank stayed behind at the field talking to the girls. The incident sparked a friendship between Frank and Jean that led to romance, and in 1954 they were married at St. Patrick's

Wedding of Frank (Teeney) Murphy to Jean Baird at St. Patrick's Church, St. John's in 1954. Kneeling: Frank Murphy, Jean (Baird) Murphy. Standing: Gus Murphy (Best Man), Father J. Murphy, Anita Baird (Maid of Honour). At railing (L-R): Patricia Murphy, Helen (Murphy) Clancey, Rose (Murphy) Jackman.

Church. At the ceremony, I sat next to Frank's brother Beaver, who was known for his quick wit and sense of humour. During the address to the gathering by Father Murphy, the priest was discussing the meaning of marriage. Father Murphy observed that, "When two people come together in marriage, they become as one." Beaver leaned over his seat and commented to Frank, "If he was outside our door when mom and dad are fighting he'd think there was a half dozen."

Frank bit his tongue to avoid breaking out into laughter and Jean gave him a scornful look. Richard (Frank's youngest brother), my brother Maurice and myself did not control our reaction and our giggling could be heard throughout the church. Now, almost forty-five years later Frank and Jean are still happily married. They have one son, Sean, and Sean and his wife Kerry have given them a grandchild, Josh.

Young people didn't seem to have as much freedom

when we were growing up as they do today. Even after boys and girls left school to go to work, parents sometimes ruled with strong discipline. I remember one night a bunch of us were hanging out near Fardy's Store (later Crotty's store, operated by Ruth and Tucker Crotty). One of the girls, Jeanette Hunt, got in a bit of a panic because it was ten minutes to eleven and she had to be home by 11:00 p.m. This seemed a late hour for us and Jeanette made it plain that she did not relish the prospect of walking home alone at that hour of the night. She lived in the east end of town.

Several of us including Andy Churchill and Betty Murphy, who later married Andy, decided to accompany Jeanette on her walk home. There was the expected clowning around and lingering and we didn't get back to Flower Hill until 11:30 p.m.. Betty Murphy, who was sixteen or seventeen at the time and had a job at Walsh's Bakery, was half an hour past her curfew. At the time we didn't know that Betty had an eleven o'clock curfew. However, seconds after she entered the front door of her house all Flower Hill knew. Her mother, Mary, was waiting on the top of the stairs for her, and the shouting could be heard all over the Hill. We learned the next day that in addition to a stiff bawling out she got a few cracks to the back of the head for not being home on time.

Word travelled fast in our neighbourhood. The next morning when Betty arrived at the Bakery for work, she was greeted at the front door by her boss, Jimmy Walsh who commented, "Well, Mary-Agnes (his nick name for her) you got a few knocks from mother Mary for being out late last night. You won't be out late tonight."

By our late teens some of the boys in our neighbourhood began experimenting with alcohol. We had no drugs to deal with but parents were always ready to counsel us on the pitfalls and danger of alcohol consumption. Still many of the boys chose to make up their own minds on the issue. Fatso Ryall belonged to the group who chose to avoid alcohol and the problems that its use could cause. But his prudent choice didn't save him from innocently getting into trouble over alcohol and the humiliation of a public arrest.

During one Christmas season, Pat Hearn and a few of the boys decided they would pick up some beer at the neighbourhood bootleggers. No sooner had the suggestion been made than Fatso spoke up, "Count me out." Pat tried to persuade him to change his mind but he remained steadfast in his resolve not to go along with them. Fatso got out of the car, and went home.

Meanwhile, Pat, Albert Brown, Justin Carey and one or two more of the boys from the neighbourhood had no trouble in purchasing a case of beer at the bootleggers. They were heading up Casey Street on their way to a place to drink it when they noticed Fatso coming out of his house. The car stopped, backed up and Pat rolled down the window. "Come on Fatso, we're going for some fish 'n' chips," he shouted. Fatso got into the car and did not notice the beer which the boys had placed behind the passenger seat.

After turning onto LeMarchant Road a police car with flashing lights and a blaring siren seemed to come out of nowhere and beckoned them to stop. The police officer conducted a quick outside inspection of the car then he turned his flashlight on the inside. He noticed the case of beer on the back seat floor. A few minutes later the Black Mariah was at the scene and the boys, with Fatso loudly protesting his innocence were escorted into the back of the van. When recalling the incident Fatso said, "I was never so embarrassed in all my life. While we were being escorted into the Black Mariah a crowd coming from the Knights of Columbus had gathered around. I didn't know that the boys had beer in the car."

They were taking to police headquarters for questioning. The police officer was asking Al Brown a series of questions and he was politely answering "Yes sir, No sir." Then in answer to one of the officers questions Al broke the intensity of the moment for everyone when he replied, "Yes sir, No sir, three bags full, sir." Not only the boys but the police officers too all broke into laughter.

Justin Carey decided to take the rap for the offence and he received a notice to appear in court the next morning. The Judge fined him $25.00 but he didn't have to pay a cent. The others chipped in about five dollars each to cover the fine.

When crabapples were in season no apple tree within a radius of three miles of our neighbourhood was safe. Boys went off in gangs to invade gardens and collect the bitter-tasting fruit. George Bartlett had one of the highest and most productive crabapple trees in the city. It was also one of the most challenging trees to access because George kept a sharp eye on his garden. In addition, he had a large black hostile mongrel dog which roamed the garden freely. But centre-town boys were known for their ingenuity. Andy Churchill and Ches Stamp developed a scheme to enable them to get into the garden, up the tree, fill their pockets with crabapples and get out again before George could catch them.

Andy and Ches would search the neighbourhood for a dog or cat. They would toss the animal over the fence and George's dog would become mesmerized in following or fighting the uninvited visitor. With the guard dog's attention diverted, Andy and Ches would retrieve as many crabapples as possible and get safely out of the garden.

The older boys in our neighbourhood often told a story that has become a legend among many downtowners. It involved Gus Murphy, Tucker Crotty, Famy Sears and a few others. Whenever there was a parade to the War Memorial on Queen's Road it always attracted the children from our neighbourhood. On one such occasion, Gus and the boys were seen carrying a bag and rushing to get to the Memorial before the parade arrived. When the crowd had gathered and the parade arrived Gus and his friends disappeared behind a house on Cathedral Street.

According to one who was there, the boys climbed to the roof of a house. Gus untied the bag and they all giggled as he retrieved its contents. Minutes later a twenty-one gun salute was called for and the guns began to fire. Bang! Bang! Bang! they fired. Then on the fourth or fifth explosion of gun-fire the boys each grabbed one of several dead pigeons which Gus had taken from the bag and threw them into the air and towards the gun fire. They then made a fast dash to get down from the roof and away from the area.

The police reacted to the practical joke and gave chase as spectators roared laughing. The boys evaded the police and made it back to Flower Hill. They were never caught, and for years after denied having anything to do with the affair. But, one who was there swears it happened and later revealed the identities of the practical jokers.

Owning a car in the 1950s was a real status symbol. The condition of the car made no difference. Horses had all but disappeared from the streets by the late 1950s. People were turning more and more to automobiles, but knew very little about them. Young men especially often bought an old wreck and just parked it by their door hoping someone would come along and get it going. These cars became prestigious neighbourhood hang outs.

Buff O'Keefe and a few of the boys once bought an old Prefect car from Harry Mullins. They paid five dollars and an

Irene Knitwear sweater for the vehicle. It had no motor but the body and interior were in excellent condition. The old Prefect was a real blessing on rainy summer days. Winst Noftle recalls that it was unbelievable how many were able to fit into the old Prefect.

I recall well one hot summer day when the boys decided to take the motorless Prefect for a joy ride. There was Buff, Dinty, Pat Hearn, Jackie Leonard, Cec Pearson, Winston Noftle, Dino Caul and one or two others. The last two in pushed the car over Central Street and when she got rolling jumped in and closed the door.

They turned left by Walsh's Bakery and left again down Casey Street. It was all downhill until they got to New Gower Street. All the way they were shouting and waving to their friends. Anyone watching the old Prefect coast down Casey Street would have thought it had a motor. It was also obvious that the occupants were having a great time cruising in a motorless automobile.

When she finally came to a stop on New Gower Street, everyone would jump out and push her back up Casey Street and over Central Street to get her ready for another cruise downtown.

The boys in our neighbourhood were a close knit group. When they graduated from high school the gang began breaking up. They had new interests, new friends, and new careers. A few even went on to University, though University was not as accessible in those days as it is today and most chose to go directly into the work force. One who chose University was Buff (Mike) O'Keefe, who went to St. Mary's University in Nova Scotia after graduating from Holy Cross.

It was a sad time when they all congregated together by Fardy's Store the night before Buff left for University. Although it was an informal gathering everyone made it a point to drop by to wish Buff well. Dinty was there to liven things up, and there was a lot of good natured ribbing taking place. "So ya going to University, Buff. What are ya gonna be, a rocket scientist?" Dinty asked. When the chuckling settled Buff explained that he was going for a Bachelor of Arts Degree. Again Dinty was off the mark with the comment, "Bachelor of Arts? Go way Buff, ya can't even draw!"

Early next morning Buff was off to St. Mary's. However, he took an immediate dislike to the place and after four days was back home in St. John's. The night of his return he went out to seek the company of his buddies who were hanging around by Walsh's Bakery chewing the fat. Buff was feeling sheepish about his first attempt at University. When Dinty saw Buff coming he turned to the rest of the boys and said loud enough for Buff to hear, ". . . and they say there's no brains in this part of town. Here comes a fellow who got his Bachelor of Arts from St. Mary's in just four days." Not to be out done Buff, who was aware of how irritated Dinty got when anyone called him by his given name Michael, patted Dinty on the head and said, "My, my little Michael how you've grown since I've been away."

Some of the boys had their own style of language. A stranger might take offence but someone who grew up in a downtown neighbourhood would have no problem with it. One example which stands out in my mind involves a good friend, Bill Philips.

When Bill encountered someone he hadn't seen in decades and couldn't remember the name, a puzzled look came over his face. He would size up the person and say, "I don't remember the name . . . but I know the f- - - - n' face." No insult was ever intended.

People who grew up in downtown St. John's in the 1940s and 1950s generally experienced hard times. This situation reflected more on the economic state of the province in that era than anything else. Now when friends from that era get together they speak about hard times experienced as one would talk about a badge of courage. In fact, they compete with each other for the claim to have experienced the most difficult times.

Frank Jackman, another lifelong friend of mine, could always top any such conversation with his gem of a claim. After a round of recollections by everyone present, Frank would state, "When I was growing up we were so poor that if I had not been born a boy, I would have had nothing to play with."

Pre-TV Era

It's hard to imagine a world without television and VCRs. Yet that was the world we grew up in until television arrived in 1955. The coming of television changed people's social lives.

In pre-television days people socialized more with their friends and neighbours. The kitchen table and the cup of tea played a major role in peoples lives, and there were frequent house parties. The chain that confines people today to their television sets and to their homes did not exist.

Among the many ways adults amused themselves during the pre-television era was the weekly card club. In just about every household someone was a member of one of these clubs. These were small groups of eight to ten who got together weekly to play a game called 120 which was always followed by 'the cup of tea.' Each member had to bring sandwiches, buns or cake for the tea and each member took a turn at hosting the event. It was the responsibility of the host to provide the prizes. The club was also a means of saving money for Christmas. At each game a small fee of one or two dollars was collected and banked. A week or so before Christmas the money would be withdrawn and paid to the members according to the contributions each made.

At one such gathering, Helen Clancey became convinced

that her brother-in-law, Frank Jackman, had to be cheating. He had been winning just about every hand of cards.

During the game, Frank excused himself from the table to go to the toilet. Water and sewer had been installed by then. He did not close the door and you could distinctly hear water hitting water as Frank relieved himself. His wife Rose, a little embarrassed, shouted, "For Christ's sake Frank close the bathroom door."

Helen, already steaming over Frank's success at cards remarked, "Leave him alone Rose. This is the first time to-night that I know what he got in his hands."

Not only were people friendlier and more neighbourly in the days before television; they were also more creative in amusing themselves. After television, people's behaviour changed drastically. Television captivated the public and slowly people began centring their lives around the boob tube. They spent more time at home and less time visiting friends or just strolling through neighbourhoods and town. The large circles of friendships dwindled as did the familiarity with the neighbourhood and its people. People slowly lost the willingness and the ability to develop large networks of neighbourhood friends and acquaintances or to make their own fun and entertainment.

In pre-TV days people left their homes more often and consequently they got to know others in and outside their neighbourhood. If you didn't know a person by name, you certainly knew them by sight. When passing in the streets people always exchanged greetings . . . "Good night, Ma'am' or "Good day, sir," were very common greetings. Jim Fardy, who operated a grocery store on Flower Hill, was one of the finest mannered gentlemen in town. He always addressed his female customers politely, and often used the phrase, "I'm graced by your presence, Ma'am" to a new lady moving into the neighbourhood. The closeness developed in the neighbourhoods of the 50s and previous years is still very evident among people today when they resume old acquaintances.

The radio was a popular source of entertainment and information but it never dominated people's lives the way television eventually did. There were floor-model as well as shelf-model radios. One floor-model had an eye-like coloured light above the station selection area. These models were referred to as the magic eye radios. There was no such thing as a transistor then; these radios were powered by tubes. When you turned on the radio it would take a minute or two for the tubes to heat up enough to carry the sound. So you could not turn your radio and hear instant sound. If you did not have the dial exactly on the station you got a lot of static. Battery powered radios were available for houses without electricity, but these were not the type you could carry around. The battery was sometimes larger than the radio. It was designed for use in the house and not as a portable.

The phonograph player was also very popular. These played records of various speeds; 33 rpm, 45 and 75 rpms. You could purchase a floor-model console that included a radio and a phonograph player. One of the most impressive in town was owned by Ches Pippy. That radio was given to an employee of Pippy and is today a valued part of the household furniture of a family on Shea Heights.

Radio provided some fine entertainment. Throughout the day there were the soaps which housewives listened to as they ploughed their way through a day of hard work. These radio soaps were as compelling listening for the housewife as todays' television soaps. However, they were very short episodes usually lasting fifteen minutes. I remember my mother demanding and expecting silence from 4:45 p.m. to 5:15 p.m. weekdays so she could keep up to date on her two favourite soaps. Ma Perkins came on at 4:45 p.m., followed by Pepper Young at 5:00 p.m. Both shows were broadcast over CBN Radio.

You could set your clock by the 5:29 p.m. Bulova Time Signal and the 6:29 p.m. Mercury Time Signal. Every day at 6.00 p.m. CBN broadcast a children's story. The most memorable of these was the Christmas Series . . . Jonathan Thomas' Christmas on the Moon. Other popular CBN shows included the Gerald S. Doyle Bulletin which came on at 7:45 p.m. and Aubrey McDonald's Heartbeat In Sports at 8:45 p.m. Other memorable CBN shows included the Kraft Music Hall, Arthur Godfrey Show and every Monday night at 7:30 p.m. there was Boston Blackie. Philo Vance, like Blackie, was another thrilling private detective show on CBN. CBN signed off each night at midnight with the Ode to Newfoundland, God Save the King, and O Canada.

The most popular radio program for children was the Uncle Harry Show. This was a live entertainment show featuring talented local children like Mary Lou Collins, Joyce Philips, Paul Sears, Diane Ring, Loretta Rideout, Terry Dwyer, Robert (Bouncer) Abbott and dozens more. The show was hosted by Harry Brown who eventually moved to CBC and hosted several national television programs. The Uncle Harry show started on CJON radio. It was carried live from an auditorium in the old Gaiety Building at Buckmaster's Circle which housed the CJON radio station. When Harry Brown moved to VOCM on McBride's Hill the Uncle Harry show went with him. VOCM had a small auditorium on the second floor of the Pope Building. In both instances Harry would invite children from the audience to come on stage and perform.

When I was eight or nine years old, I responded to Harry's invitation for someone to come on stage and perform. I walked up to the stage and after a few minutes chatting with Harry, he asked what I was going to do, sing or play the piano? I answered, "I'm going to tap dance." I knew instinctively by the look on Harry's face that he had not anticipated this type of situation . . . dancing on radio. His perplexed look quickly changed to a controlled grin as he explained the listeners could not see a dancer. I had tap shoes on and suggested they could listen to the taps. The idea amused Harry. Evan Johnson played the piano accompaniments for this show and I asked him to play "The Irish Washerwoman." I then went on to dance the entire five sets of steps of "The Irish Washerwoman." It was the first, last and only time Uncle Harry allowed a tap dancer on his show.

Paul Rumsey: Paul was a Newfoundland singing sensation in the 1950s. He was among the stars of the Uncle Harry radio show, and went on to lead his own very popular band, The Ravens.

VOCM featured some fine radio programs as well. On Saturday mornings there was the J.M. Devine's Big Six show which featured Newfoundland and Irish music. Devine owned the Big Six Department store at 339 Water Street. His slogan was "The Big Six, Once a number, now an institution." VOCM featured two very popular soaps: Young Doctor Malone, 11:00 a.m. to 11:15 a.m., and the Guiding Light from 12:00 to 12:15 p.m. Two other popular VOCM shows were the Spelling B, a live local broadcast, and Church In The Wildwood. Both were aired on Friday nights. Bob McLeod, the organist at the Presbyterian Kirk on Queen's Road, was a very popular local personality who had a nightly show on VOCM called Melodies by McLeod. He was known for his musical talents and as an after dinner speaker. VO's most popular children's program next to the Uncle Harry Show was the Cisco Kid on Tuesday's at 7:30 p.m. In 1949 VOCM signed off the air at 11:00 p.m.

The best and most popular radio shows, it seems, came from VOUS, the American station which operated from Fort Pepperrel, now Pleasantville. There lineup included great shows like: Life of Riley, Al Jolson, Dragnet, Our Miss Brooks, Blondie, Red Skeleton, the Whistler, Fibber McGee and Molly, and Passing Parade. All these were broadcast on Friday nights. Sporting fans would be glued to their radio sets on Saturday afternoons listening to live baseball games from the U.S. on VOUS.

Our only knowledge of television came from what we saw on the movie screens at the movie theatres around town. When my cousin Don Carew invited me to go to his sister Shirley's on Southside Road to see her television set I eagerly agreed. Shirley was married to an American serviceman and had returned to St. John's from living in the United States. She brought her household furniture with her and that included a television set.

Once inside the house Don wasted no time in ushering me into the living room to see the television. We were both in awe. We inspected it from top to bottom, touched it, looked behind it and then asked Shirley to turn it on. We were disillusioned when she explained to us the set could not work here because we had no television stations in Newfoundland. Nevertheless, we had seen our first real television set and were able to boast to our friends about the experience.

Several years later television came to St. John's when in 1955 CJON television went on the air. At first very few people had television sets. When someone in a neighbourhood purchased one it had an unusual impact on neighbours, friends and relatives. CJON signed on around 4:30 p.m. with a test pattern and programming began at 5:00 p.m. Throughout the evening the house would fill to overflowing, and people even crowded around kitchen and living room windows peering in to get a glimpse of a television show. Maud and Tom Walsh were the first in the Charlton Street and Coronation Street area to have a set and for months they had crowds to deal with almost every night, but especially on Friday nights for professional wrestling with Whipper Billy Watson, Hard Boiled Haggerty, the Burnetti Brothers and other top names at the time.

It was common to see people throughout the City standing outside looking into a house window at a television set. It was even more common to see people, often whole families, after supper head for Water Street. Televisions in department store windows were left on to demonstrate the new appliance and entice people to purchase one. By 7:30 p.m. it was difficult to find a good spot in front of any of the windows.

People were amazed at the ability of Don Jamieson to give a full newscast including, local, national and international news without having to read or refer to any written script. People who worked with CJON at the time explained that Don had a photographic memory. He simply read a prepared newscast before going on air. He then put the papers aside and delivered the news of the day. The public loved him. Jamieson also hosted a series of local entertainment shows and his Christmas Eve with the Jamieson's was looked forward to each Christmas. On that show Don brought the cameras into his home and, surrounded by his wife Barbara and their children, he would read "The Night Before Christmas."

I recall in 1956 what I believe to be the first television contest in Newfoundland. It was a jingle contest sponsored by Val Earle Distributor's to promote a powdered milk product called Milko. The program was announced on the Greg Bonner Show, seen every evening at 6 p.m. on CJON-TV. It was a half hour show, which featured a variety of short cowboy movies and included such names as Tom Mix, Hop-a-Long Cassidy, Gene Autrey, Roy Rogers, Cisco Kid, Lash Larue and others.

The prize attracted the interest of every young boy within range of the broadcast. The Ford Motor Company had made a dozen or so small 1956 red Thunderbirds for promotion in Canada and the United States. The battery powered car was about five feet long, thirty inches wide and could travel at twelve miles per hour. The Greg Bonner show was very popular among kids and when the car was offered as a prize it seemed everyone was trying their hand at writing jingles, hoping to win the Thunderbird convertible.

My mother was very good at writing verses and jingles and by then had won dozens of radio contests on both CJON and VOCM. CJON Radio had a daily Big Mike contest in which they awarded a pen with a big mike on it to the best jingle of the day promoting CJON. She must have won dozens of these. My brother Maurice and I always had one to take to school. In another contest for a giant Mechano set on CJON radio she wrote a jingle which won me the prize. Of course, she would always sign either my name or my brother's to her entries.

She penned a half dozen Milko jingles and chose the one she considered best to enter the contest. It seemed that the Thunderbird was the daily conversation among my friends at school and many of them had entered as well. On the day the winner was announced we were all excited and hoping to hear our name read out by Greg Bonner as contest winner.

I was watching the show as usual and when time came to pick the winner I noticed that Bonner was holding a very large brown envelope. My heart sank. I thought, "My entry was in a regular white envelope. I'm not the winner." Then he read the winner's name and I thought it must be another Jack Fitzgerald, until he added the address. There was no doubt, I had won the Thunderbird. I appeared on the Greg Bonner show the next night where a representative of the sponsoring company passed me the keys. I had to wait several days though, until CJON could arrange delivery of the vehicle. Crowds of kids gathered in front of my house on Charlton Street when John Nolan, a broadcaster with CJON at that time delivered the prize to my door during his live Saturday afternoon road show.

I never got to drive the car. It was carried up over a set of five or six steps and stored in our front hallway. It was too big and heavy for me to take out. Eventually, my uncle, Frank Fitzgerald purchased it from me and placed it on tickets at the Holy Cross Pantry Shelf to raise money for the school. I believe the car was won by a Mr. Harding on Pleasant Street. I don't know what happened to it after that. I didn't really care at the time, because I had used the money from the sale to buy a new three speed bicycle with saddle bags and a horn.

While my mother wrote a scrapbook full of jingles which won a variety of prizes over the years, none have survived. I do however, have a copy of a song she wrote for the 1966 Come Home Year. It was written to be sung to the tune of "Auld Lang Syne" and was published in the Newfoundland Bulletin.

The year is 1966 and our slogan is come home
All you Newfoundlanders who have left our shores to roam.
Vacation time is here again, so why not take this stand,
To pack your grip, and take a trip, back home to
        Newfoundland.

You'll find there's many changes here, our province it
        has grown
Since the day, you sailed away, to a home away from home.
But now the time has come when you should visit us
        once more
We'll welcome you with open arms and help you
        rant and roar.

If fishing is your favourite sport, then come back home
        you ought,
Our brooks and ponds are filled with fish just
        waiting to be caught.
Conception Bay with tuna teems, so bring a friend or two,
Our forests green, with big game teem such as
        moose and caribou.

Then you'll drive out over TCH and view the sights so grand
You won't find many pretty sights, like we have in
        Newfoundland.
And when vacation time is o'er and you'll leave our
        shores far behind
Please take with you, our blessings true, for the sake of
        Auld Lang Syne.

Olden Days' Summer Fun

When I look back on summertime fun in the St. John's of my youth, it seems like every day was a model summer day with brilliant sunshine, cloudless skies and a refreshing ocean breeze. It may be that with age, we remember only the best, or perhaps the weather was really better in the 1940s and 1950s.

There was no shortage of places to go, things to do, or new things to experience. The concrete tombs of chlorine-polluted water we now call swimming pools existed only on the movie screens. The natural swimming holes like Sandy Bottom and Capsules near Bowring Park; Sugar Loaf in the east end; Twin Falls in Mount Pearl and Manuels with its Canyon and Flats were frequented by not only the youth of the city but everyone.

Most city streets were unpaved and the highways out of the city were still unpaved. Very few families owned cars and most people relied on the bus for transportation. There was the Golden Arrow, replaced by Capitol Coach Ltd., for transportation around the City, and several fleets of "Yellow Busses" as we knew them to take travellers to fields, meadows and fishing holes outside the city. There was the Petty Har-

Kozy Korner-Located at the intersection of New Gower Street and Lime Street. Lee's Petty Harbour Bus operated from this site.

bour Bus operated by J.J. Lee; Petten's Bus operated a service between St. John's and Kelligrew's, and Evans' Busses operated between St. John's and Pouch Cove.

A common practice in those days was for entire neighbourhoods to band together for a Sunday outing. Everyone chipped in to pay the rental fee for a yellow bus or a truck, and each family brought its own food supplies for the boil-up. Popular outing places included Fourth Pond, Manuels, Midstream (adjacent to Bowring Park) and for the Flower Hill neighbourhood there was Maloney's Meadow in Mount Pearl. This meadow was huge enough for the men and boys to play soccer while the ladies tended to the food preparation. Some of those who made these country excursions were Jack Anthony and Jim Fardy (they usually organized the events), Mike Murphy, Billy Woods, Tucker Crotty, the Sears boys, Beaver Murphy, the Abbotts, Max Taylor, Kevin (Stuarty) Taylor, Walshes, Malones, the Murphy brothers from both sides of Flower Hill, the Leonards, Dago Janes, Pat and Mike (Dinty) Hearn, Scotts, O'Briens, Fowlers, Whelans, Cauls, Edneys, Roaches and Kinsellas and so on. While darkness descended over the field everyone gathered around a central camp fire. The smaller boys and girls who were too young to join in the activities of the older crowd spent hours combing the woods for blasty boughs for the big fire. Jack Anthony would play the accordion and everyone would join in the

Cub Scouts: Jack Fitzgerald is shown here standing on the extreme right. Kneeling on the extreme left is Pat Hearn. Third from the left (standing next to Fitzgerald) is David Edison and Bill Neville. Kneeling is Jack Murphy. Top extreme left (standing) is Bouncer Abbott. Third from top left is Pat Murphy.

sing-a-long with songs like *Forever and Ever, Four Leaf Clover, Cheating Heart, If I were a Blackbird.* Whether by truck or bus, the trip to and from the picnic spot was always fun. There would be a lot of singing and joking around throughout the ride to and from the Meadow.

From the first of June until Labour Day weekend, Manuels was a literal tent city. People didn't go far from the city in those days to enjoy the country. Some people had the good fortune to have summer homes. But they were never referred to as summer homes. They were simply called shacks. Sometimes several families in a neighbourhood would pool their resources to build such a shack. Families who didn't have shacks would rush to Manuels in early June in order to assure a good spot to erect their tent. The tent would be left up all summer in most cases and men often commuted to work by bus living out of these tents. In those days, with very few car owners, Manuels was considered a good distance from the city.

Meanwhile, we had excellent freshwater swimming pools supervised by the City at: Rennies River, Bowring Park, Victoria Park and Quidi Vidi. In those days you would see a scene at every bus stop along LeMarchant Road that you would never dream of seeing today. Around mid-day kids would head for the bus stops along that route to catch a bus to Bowring Park, the most popular park and swimming pool in the City. It was not at all unusual to see a large crowd of kids gathered at each and every stop along that road. It cost ten cents to get a bus ride to the park and the busses left Parade Street every fifteen minutes. The first few busses were generally loaded to capacity. Every seat had several kids crammed onto it, and every available inch of standing room was taken up. These busses went straight to the park, passing the hordes of kids waiting at the bus stops along the way.

A tranquil summer afternoon at the Bowring Park boat pool c.1950. This pool is now given over for the exclusive use of the park's swans and ducks.

Those in the bus jeered the kids standing at the stops with their swimming suits wrapped in towels and held under their arms. Sometimes, in anticipation of the jeering, some of the rowdier children would throw stones at the passing bus, trying earnestly to hit anyone in a window.

Arrival of the busses at the Park was a sight to see. Kids poured out of the bus in wild anticipation of a great day. The park was far more beautiful than it is today. The boat pond, as we called it, had more water in it. The island had a small house on it that sometimes housed a couple of monkeys. There were free boat rides and there was always a line-up at the wharf near the Peter Pan statue for that treat. There was usually a supervisor or two on the wharf. He would allow the oldest or most mature person in a group to take a boat out and be responsible for rowing it. When time was up these supervisors would give a hand signal and the boats would return to drop off their passengers and prepare for a new departure.

From there it was on to the swimming pool. This was a

The old Bowring Park swimming pool at the dam.

City of St. John's Archives A802 1.12.004

Bowring Park Swimming Pool-1950s.

swimming area formed by damning the river flowing down through the Park. The sides were constructed of concrete and there were diving boards and a high dive at the men's pool. The men's pool was the first pool near the dam. The river was divided in sections by thick ropes into a mens, ladies, teens and babies pool. There were bathing houses on both sides of the pool.

If one wanted more adventure he could choose a hike up to the Capsules swimming hole about a half mile upstream from the pool. This however, required a walk through thick woods, high grass, muddy banks, a shallow river, and over rugged banks. Nevertheless, Capsules was a very popular swimming hole. It afforded some of the more daring a chance to show off their diving skills by diving from a high cliff at top of the falls flowing into the hole. This was popular despite the danger of diving from cliffs in unsupervised swimming areas.

A gruesome accident occurred in 1955 or 1956 at a swimming hole in Manuels called the Canyon. It was a typical hot summer's day and the area was crowded with young boys and girls swimming and playing in the water. Several boys began diving from the cliff overlooking the swimming hole. The swimming area was rather small. The water ran down from Paddy's Pond and entered at the Canyon between two high walls of rock. The pool may have stretched twenty feet wide. Most kids were aware of the several large rocks beneath the surface and the danger they posed.

A boy new to the area joined in with some of the experienced kids diving from the cliff about twenty-five feet above the water. Unaware of the danger below the boy, about thirteen or fourteen, dived into the water head first and struck one of the submerged rocks. The pool suddenly turned red with his blood. Two adults in the area pulled the unconscious boy from the water and placed him in a resting position. Several of the older boys were sent to fetch medical help from a doctor's clinic in Manuels. The boy had to be taken down river on a stretcher for about a quarter of a mile

City of St. John's Archives c231 5.07.028

Bowring Park Bungalow taken in the 1950s

and placed in an ambulance which took him to the General Hospital at St. John's. He recovered from the accident but was paralysed from the neck down. It was some time before many of the kids there that day ever returned to the Canyon.

Sandy Bottom was also in Bowring Park but on the opposite side of Capsules. To get there you would walk up the track and past the Bungalow for about five minutes. Sandy Bottom, was much smaller than Capsules. There were no falls to dive from, just a picturesque secluded area with a refreshing swimming hole.

A black American serviceman named Barney was the most magnificent swimmer I have ever seen. Whenever Barney went swimming in the Bowring Park Pool his unique style of swimming attracted an audience. His was a distinctive, graceful style which many tried to imitate. He would move back and forth across the pool using a technique similar to the Australian Crawl. However, as each hand in turn cut into the water his body would arch and follow the downward direction until he disappeared. Then twenty or thirty feet away his hand would penetrate the water's surface in an upward motion and he would appear again to take another disappearing cut of the water. Barney needed only two or three strokes to cross the pool. It seemed he was in continuous action for very long periods of time. Sometimes he would just swim under water and we would stand on shore guessing out loud where and when he would come up. He could hold his breath underwater longer than any other person using the pool.

When we arrived at the pool each day we would rush to change in the bathing houses which were constructed adjacent to and on both sides of the pool so we could get in the water before Barney left. He always had time for the kids and would oblige giving some swimming tips whenever we were fortunate enough to corner him.

I was particularly thankful for Barney's presence at the pool one very hot summer's day in 1952. That year I entered the swimming races at the pool. The starting point was the dam. Participants had to stand on the dam, wait for the whistle then dive in and swim to the ropes separating the men's pool from the next section. In retrospect, it was a dangerous practice, which very likely would not be tolerated today. We were a group of nine and ten-year-olds standing on a dam from which if we fell backward would have dropped about six feet onto a shallow covered area. However, that possibility never entered our minds.

Crowds had gathered on both sides of the pool to watch the competition. We stood in a ready position and when I heard the whistle I dived head first into the water. I considered myself a pretty good swimmer at that age; I had learned the Australian crawl and the breast stroke from Bridey Cole at Victoria Park. Bridey was a park worker known and loved by every child in the west end. Yet, once in the water I decided that instead of doing the crawl I would easily win by switching to Barney's style of swimming. The name we used for showing off in those days was 'gatching' and I was certainly gatching when I tried to emulate Barney.

I got off a few good strokes and was moving rhythmically through the waters. I glanced towards the spectators and swallowed water. This broke my pace, threw me off and I began to choke. I panicked. Unable to call for help, I splashed around in the water. I had not noticed Barney among the spectators earlier but he was there. In seconds he was in the water at my side. He grabbed me and held me above water until I got my breath then he pulled me safely to shore. I didn't win any prizes that day but being saved by Barney was something that I treasured far more than any of the medals that my friends won.

But swimming was only one summertime activity. Most of our fun took place on the streets around our homes. On one hot day when things got a little boring, I was influenced by Spuds (God forbid) to climb up on the roof of his house. We were living on Charlton Street that year and once on the roof we had a spectacular view of Southside and the harbour. Spuds had no fear of heights—but as I discovered that day, I did!

Downtown houses were and still are joined together which made it possible for us to walk along the roofs on Charlton Street as far as Churchill's on Coronation Street. We could go no further there because of a laneway between Churchill's and Greenland's. On the way back it was pure devilment that caused us to stop and pour a half bottle of Pepsi down a chimney. We didn't know, or care whose chimney it was at the time.

Minutes later we heard an uproar down on Charlton Street. The fearless Spuds went to the edge of the roof to look down. I remained in the middle roof area away from the view of the street.

Spuds commented, "There's something wrong down on the street. There's a crowd around Mrs. Evans and she's covered in soot,like Aunt Jemima." When the crowd got a glimpse of Spuds on the roof Mrs. Evans angrily shouted something to Spuds. He came in from the edge and said, "We better get outa here. I think she's mad at us." When we got down from the roof we learned that Mrs. Evans had been cleaning her kitchen coal stove when we poured the Pepsi down her chimney causing the soot to become airborne and covering her from head to foot. She didn't know what was happening so she ran out into the street for help.

Fortunately, they had not seen me on the roof. Mrs. Evans went to Spuds' mother and told her that he had been on her roof and had thrown something down the chimney. Spuds was punished severely. Spuds didn't tell on me so I escaped punishment, and my role in the incident was never uncovered.

Soon after Confederation, with the influx of Canadian dollars, the city was transformed. The first outward signs of this change was the extensive paving of city Streets. Most streets had no pavement and no paved sidewalks. When the steam rollers and council workers moved into our neighbourhood to pave the streets they attracted many spectators. I was among the crowds that stood nearby and watched the first paving of Casey Street. The tar-making machine had a special appeal for the children. I don't know who or where the practice of chewing pitch started but it was widespread. Pitch was the black tar caked to the sides of the tar machine. We would break off pieces and share them with our friends. We chewed this pitch like children today chew gum. I don't remember anyone ever getting sick from the practice and it had a cleansing effect on our teeth.

Frogs make poor pets, yet young boys always managed during summer holidays to capture and keep one—at least until it was discovered by a parent and quickly evicted. Kevin Rumsey of Lime Street was no exception. At the age of ten he captured a frog from a gully near St. John's and brought it home. His intentions were to keep it as a pet. Then one day while in the garden showing how far it could leap it escaped. The garden was filled with piles of uncut wood and it easily found a hiding place.

Kevin and his friends searched the garden over and over without success. Each day he would go out into the garden and look around but as the days went by he lost interest and soon forgot the frog.

September came and school reopened. Then fall followed by winter with its snowstorms and frost and finally the warm weather of spring arrived melting the winter snow.

Kevin and his brothers went to the garden to sort out the wood for chopping. As they worked they heard a noise which at first they didn't recognize. Then it became more frequent. When they moved the wood from the position where the sound was coming from they were amazed to see the little frog of the previous summer. He had not only survived the harsh cold winter but obviously had flourished and grown to a much larger size.

Another neighbourhood boy had a repulsive experience with a very different type of animal. Children could have their pick of a large variety of toys at Brookfield Ice Cream on Lemarchant Road. All we had to do was collect Brookfield popsicle, or fudgesicle wrappers. Brookfield passed out catalogues with prize lists and the number of wrappers needed to purchase each item.

Children walked around the streets picking up wrappers or rescuing discarded ones from garbage cans. Some even swapped their wrappers with others in return for comic books or double bubble gum. One young boy from Cabot Street collected enough wrappers to purchase a hunting knife.

While walking home from the ice cream plant with a group of friends, he came across a dazed rat at the top of Springdale Street. The rat was either sick or dying from rat poison. The boy, about twelve years old and fearless, crept up behind the rat; seized it by the tail and tossed it into the air. Then as it spiralled towards the ground he speared it with his knife. He was not daunted by the spectacle, but his friends were stomach sick for days.

Children could always find something interesting to do. When not attending movies or going "off for a swim," there were many children's street games that were played. The boys played: Head on the Roost, Snatch the Hanky, Boggers, Box Ball, Soccer, Baseball, Softball and Street Hockey. The girls had games like Hop Scotch, Skipping, Eenie Clapsie, Cat's Cradle and Jacks. Both boys and girls would join together to play Tin Tacks, Simon Says, Hoist Your Sails and Run, Kick the Can, and Piddly Sticks.

I remember many a summer's morning when living on Charlton Street being awakened by the girls on the street playing skipping. My bedroom was on the front of the house and with the window opened all the street noise poured in and filled the room. The girls in the neighbourhood knocked around together and played together. There were Ruth and Stella Squires, Brenda Evans, Mary Neville, Joan and Kay Handrigan, Anne Harding, Roz Cook, Dot Janes, Evelyn Harris and Jennifer Greenland.

One of the skipping chants I often awoke to was:

> Ruthie in the kitchen,
> doing a bit of stitchin',
> In come's Mary and
> pushes her out.

In this game the girl whose name is mentioned jumps into the skipping area and pushes the other girl out. Another skipping game they played was Peel-a-Banana:

Peel a banana upside down.
Peel an orange round and round.
If you count to twenty-four,
You can have your turn once more,
One, two, ... twenty-four.

If you skipped to twenty-four without tripping the rope you got another turn.

The girls also played some hand-clapping games. One which was popular was **My Boyfriend's Name**

Oh I'm a funny little Dutchgirl
As funny as funny can be, be, be,
And all the boys down our way
Are very fond of me, me, me.

My boyfriend's name is Yellow
He comes from Yellabellow
With a big fat nose
And buckles on his toes
And you should hear him
Laugh laugh, laugh.

Come listen to my story
@POEM = A story that is true,
And if you want to marry me
I'll tell you what to do, do, do.

Just fill your pockets with money
And take me to the show
And take me to the pictures
Wherever, you should go, go, go.

Another clapping game was Peas Pudding Hot:

> Peas puddin' hot
> Peas puddin' cold.
> Peas puddin' in the pot,
> Nine days old.
>
> Some like it hot,
> Some like it cold.
> Some like it in the pot,
> Nine days old.

The boys liked the snatch-a-hanky game. This involved two teams of equal number, and a referee. Each team faced-off from opposite sides of the street. Before starting the referee would go to each player and give him a number, usually one to five if only five were on each team. Each team had a set of numbers one to five.

The referee would go to the middle of the street. When he raised the hanky in the air all the players would get set, in anticipation of their number being called. He would then drop the hanky and call a number from one to five. The player on each side with that number would face the challenge of running out, picking up the hanky and getting back to his own starting point (ghoulous) without being touched by the other player. If the other player touched you when you had the hanky in your hand it was a point for the opposing side. If you got the hanky to ghoulous without being tagged your team got a point.

Head-on-the-roost was another popular game. One player would brace himself against a wall and another player would bend forward and wrap his hands tightly around the person standing. The players would then line up and one at a time would run and jump on the back of the player or players bending over. As he ran he would shout one, two three head-on-the-roost for me. When there was not enough room for a jumper to land he would become the next link in the roost. The game would end when there was no room left on the roost for another player.

In choosing players for each game we would use rhymes to pick a player. One such rhyme was My Mother and Your Mother:

My mother and your mother were hanging out clothes
My mother gave your mother a punch in the nose.
And guess what colour the blood came out?

Whoever you pointed to had to say a colour. The person doing the selecting would then spell out the colour, pointing to a player with each letter and the person being pointed to at the last letter would make it on a team or side.

Everyone seemed to know the **Chinese Alphabet**. At least that was what we called it. One kid would say to another, "Do you know the Chinese Alphabet?" If the answer was no, he would then recite it.

I die, dick a die, dick a die doe knee
Ump, bump, boney,
Ala mana whisky
Chinese chum.

A verse children used to taunt their friends was **The Whooping Cough Verse**. It went:

Ah hum. Ah hum !
Me mother is gone to church

She told me not to play
    with you,
Cause you are in the lurch.
It isn't cause your dirty,
It isn't cause your clean,
It's cause you got
    the Whooping Cough
From eating Margarine.

A favourite summer game for the boys was box ball. Boys went from neighbourhood to neighbourhood to play other teams. One such game took place on Central Street in front of Walsh's Bakery in the evening after the bakery had closed. There were no bats, gloves or equipment needed to play this game—just a ball. In every other aspect it resembled baseball or softball. The same number of players, same positions, the same three bases and scoring system. In this game Peter Byrne had brought a team from the west end to play Fatso Ryall, Dinty Hearn, Fluke Noftle and their team from the Flower Hill Area.

The game was tied up going into the seventh inning when Byrne's team went out to play the field. Dinty was in his glory. He was pitching and hitting a great game and the boys were confident of victory. When Dinty stepped to the batter's plate to start off the inning Peter and the west enders formed into a huddle. Then without any warning they turned and ran away. When Dinty realized they were running away from the game he lost his temper. Like Popeye in a fit of anger you could see the colour in Dinty's face change to blood red. He took chase, shouting insults at Byrne and his players all the way. He didn't stop until he got to Byrne's house on Alexander Street where Peter escaped him by going in and closing the door. Peter and the boys knew Dinty well and had staged the incident to get his goat, which they did.

Dinty was a colourful character who could bring life and laughter to any situation, and those who knew him loved and respected him for this. Brian Healy recalled, "Even as a very young boy Dinty showed a macho type of wit. He came home one day with a black eye. His father, asked, 'Who gave ya the black eye?' Dinty replied, 'Nobody gave it to me, I had to fight for it.'"

Dinty Hearn is best remembered for his wit and humour. Anyone who knew him well knew better than to get into exchanging barbs with him. It mattered little whether it was male or female; if you threw out the challenge you had to be prepared for what he might toss back.

I recall an occasion at Bessie O'Keefe's store on McFarlane Street when boys and girls from the neighbourhood had crammed inside drinking soft drinks and chatting. Dinty was about sixteen at the time and had just started to cultivate a moustache. One of the girls with raised eyebrows, and obviously attempting a put down commented to him, "What are you trying to do, grow a moustache?" Before anyone reacted all eyes and ears focused on Dinty and we were not disappointed.

Dinty responded, "Why not? You did."

When he passed away a decade ago Caul's Funeral Home was filled to capacity. Friends he had made over the years from the neighbourhood and school had gathered to pay their last respects. Fatso Ryall recalled, "Everyone there had a Dinty story to tell." There's no doubt he touched all our lives and he is sadly missed.

Winter wonderland

The streets of St. John's became a children's playground in the winter time. The first heavy snowfall left the streets transformed into an exotic winter wonderland. There was always a danger in playing in the streets but it was less risky in those days than today because the automobile had not come into its own. This was the era of transition. The horse, which had been the main means of road transportation, was giving way to motorized vehicles, but horse-drawn wagons and carts were still being used by commercial establishments in the City.

The bakeries, soft drink companies, coal companies, grocery stores, meat markets, furniture stores and so on, all had their stable of horses and wagons which they housed in barns around the City. In the winter they would put away their wheeled carts and replace them with sleighs. These horse-drawn delivery sleighs with their tinkling bells added to the mystic and quaint atmosphere of the city streets.

The streets were rarely cleared completely of snow as happens with today's snow clearing. After the first winter's storm the white snow-topped covering of our streets would remain until spring. It was an advantage to the horse domi-

Flower Hill after a snow storm in January, 1959. L-R: Fred Barela, John Barela and Rick Barela.

nated transportation of the city to have the streets snow covered. The automobile had a more difficult time. Technology was not as advanced as it is today, and drivers depended on the manual choke to start their cars in freezing temperatures.

Faulty chokes and dead batteries discouraged many from using the automobile in wintertime. Snow tires were not yet developed and motorists used chains over their back tires to get them through the slippery streets. Frequently, the links in these chains would break and the broken chain would pound against the metal of the car in rapid fire as the car sped along the road. This loud banging sound was in contrast to the tingling of the sleigh bells on the horse-drawn sleighs.

An amusing story was often told about a police officer and an accident involving a truck and a horse. The horse was killed in the misfortune which occurred on Waldegrave Street. The police officer on the beat had a particular problem with spelling. When he arrived on the scene he was required to write a report on the incident. In writing his report he made several attempts to spell Waldegrave Street without success. Placing his pencil and notebook back in his pocket, he solicited the help of several spectators and dragged the horse thirty or forty feet to George Street. He took out pencil and paper and completed his report. He had no problem spelling George Street.

Sliding was the most popular winter entertainment. It cost little or nothing and you could do it in your own neighbourhood. Every hill and street grade in town became a sliding hill and every street a skating rink or hockey surface. City streets were crowded at night with people of all ages enjoying themselves. For sliding there was a variety of contraptions one could use. The most common was the coaster or slide, purchased at one of the Water Street stores.

I remember getting one from Freddy Best's Hardware Store on Waldegrave Street. It was a model called Champion, the strongest and most durable model in use which made it also the most popular. These coasters were made of wood and aluminum and measured about three feet long and eighteen inches wide. Each had a metal runner which gave it speed when travelling downhill. There was also a wooden bar or handle across the front with a rope tied to both ends.

The driver would sit to the rear of the slide with his passenger in front of him. He would then pull the rope attached to the steering rod over the passengers head and away they would go. He steered the coaster like a driver steered his horse. A pull on the rope to the left would turn the coaster left; a pull to the right would move it right. Your feet acted as the brakes.

When you wanted to stop you dropped your two feet onto the snow to slow the coaster until it came to a stop. In cases where you needed to stop instantly you just rolled off the slide and let it go freely until it stopped or hit something. We sometimes used this technique when approaching an intersection and someone shouted, "Horse coming."

The older boys in the neighbourhood often constructed a catamaran. This was a large contraption a little smaller than a horse sleigh but much larger than the ordinary coaster, and could carry a half dozen or more passengers. It was higher off the ground, and wider than the coaster. Only rarely did such a home made slide have a metal covering over the runners. Sometimes, a winter horse sleigh would be converted into a catamaran.

Another innovation was the home-made bob sleigh. I remember an impressive one built by Frank (Teeney) Murphy, Bill (Tucker) Crotty and Harry (Har) Constantine. It was a two-part vehicle. The front was separate from the rear which joined to it like a caboose on a train. The front had two skis which were turned by an old steering wheel taken from a scrapped car.

Kids who didn't have a slide were not the least deterred. They could double up with others, or they could grab a cardboard box, a wooden coke box, or a tin Pepsi sign, all of which travelled just as well over a slippery surface. It was not at all uncommon to see kids sliding down Flower Hill on a snow shovel.

Hill sliding was popular in all areas of town and the adults participated as willingly as the children. I remember we often sought out the challenges of other, steeper hills. We branched out to Barter's Hill, Carter's Hill, Lime Street and even Long's Hill. However, it was not always wise to move outside your own neighbourhood. The boys hung out in gangs; the Flower Hill Boys, the Cabot Street Boys and so on. One or two outsiders using their hill was not a problem. But if a gang of boys with slides came into a neighbourhood area it was perceived as a challenge to the resident gang and very likely would erupt into a snowball fight or worse.

The Flower Hill run—as far as we were concerned—was the best sliding turf in the City. It started from the intersection of Cabot Street and ran down to New Gower Street. To get to New Gower Street however, we had to make a left turn at the intersection of Casey Street and Flower Hill. It was only the odd daredevil though, who took the turn to New Gower Street. This was a dangerous practice because there was far more automobile activity on New Gower Street at night than on the side streets. One of the contrasts between city streets of our modern era with those prior to the mid-1950s is the disappearance of street sliding as a winter time recreation. In the 1950s and before, street sliding was part of the charm of city life.

When businesses closed for the day, usually 6 p.m., the horses were housed in their stables. Since there were few motor cars, and few horses on the roads at night, the streets were relatively safe. I do recall however, several tragedies in which children were run over by cars while sliding on the streets. A young boy named Robert Martin was killed by a car while sliding on Mullock or William Street in the early 1950s.

Those who didn't want to slide or tired of it would put on their skates and go to the level streets like, Central, John, Monroe and Clifford Streets to skate or play hockey. There was always a patch of ice available, or the snow itself might be smooth and hard enough for good skating. However, most street hockey games were not played on skates. These games were very competitive and players took them very seriously. Jerome 'Trapper' Gillett found this out when he first tried his hand at goal tending. While playing on Buff O'Keefe's team he hardly stopped a shot on goal from players like Fatso Ryall, Pat Hearn, Jack Leonard, Steve March, Bob and Mike

Kinsella, Mick and Bill Abbott, Pat and Mike Murphy, Cec Pearson and Jimmy Caul.

After Trapper was shut out by the opposing team in his first game, his team mates lifted him on their shoulders then tossed him over a concrete wall adjacent to Walsh's Bakery where he landed in a large bank of snow. Trapper's next game was very different. This time Fatso and the boys tried everything to score but they couldn't get the puck past Trapper. Why the dramatic change in such a short period of time? The secret was in the way he dressed. Trapper began wearing a large heavy overcoat and a fur hat.

Fatso Ryall recalled that nothing got past that overcoat. Fatso said, "Trapper would squat in front of the goal and when a shot was taken he would open his arms and the puck would disappear into the coat. Sometimes, we looked everywhere for the puck to continue the game only to see it eventually drop out of the lining or a pocket of Trapper's bloody big coat." It was during these games that Buff O'Keefe gave Gillett his nick-name ... 'Trapper.' Gillett explained that, "Buff called me Trapper because he said I dressed like a trapper during the games." The name has stuck with Jerome since then.

Small children who wanted to go skating would strap coasters onto their feet. These were aluminum skates which strapped over your footwear and had four sharp blades, two in front and two in back. This made it easy to stand on so that skating was not much of a challenge. They were used mainly as trainers for the very young who wanted to skate but couldn't stand up on real skates.

There were several outdoor skating rinks in the city. I remember going to the one behind Curtis Academy and the one behind the Prince of Wales School which was then on LeMarchant Road. There was also an indoor roller rink—But-

Courtesy Jean Murphy

Curtis Academy outdoor rink, 1952.

ler's—on Rankin Street which we went to in the wintertime. Very few people owned roller skates in those days. You rented them at the rink and returned them at the end of the session.

The end of the Christmas season provided another opportunity for winter fun. There were no artificial trees in those days—everyone used the real tree. When Christmas ended, these would be thrown outdoors for the City to collect and cart off to the dump. We would get together in a gang and decide to build a bough house. The boys would spread out all over the neighbourhood retrieving trees. We had three favourite spots in the Flower Hill area: Murphy's garden at the corner of Flower Hill and Central Street; the meadow behind Hearn's on Caul's Lane; and Cooper's Lane off Central Street just east of Flower Hill.

But, we were not the only kids out to build a bough house.

Kids in every neighbourhood shared the same interest. This often led to confrontations. These were relatively harmless clashes. Each gang would stake out an area, build a snow barricade, and stock up on snow balls. Then the snow ball fight would start. Usually the snow fort with a well stocked supply of ammunition would start the battle. It would end when one side or the other got tired of throwing the snowballs. We would grab what trees we could and drag them back to our building site. There the boys worked with hammer, saw and hatchet. First, we chopped off the boughs and piled them up, then sawed the wood into pieces to fit a frame. Then the building would start. Everyone had a job to do. These forts became the place to hang out, at least for the month of January. Usually, boys from another neighbourhood would raid and tear down the fort when the other gang was elsewhere.

During March, when the frost had really set in, there was horse racing at Quidi Vidi Lake. Although these never attracted the crowds that are traditional with the Regatta there was always several thousand spectators.

I witnessed my first horse race on the Pond on St. Paddy's Day, 1949, just days before my sixth birthday. My father and Uncle Frank took me, my brother Maurice and cousin Frank Jr. to Quidi Vidi to see the legendary Joey Judge race. I had no idea who Judge was or why he was legendary. It was exciting just to be there and see the spectacle of horses hitched to race wagons racing over the historic lake. Judge, a veteran of World War I, was then eighty-three years old with a long record of race wins, and was still racing horses. Judge had a driver for his horse, but he also raced him in several of the races and was successful. Whenever Judge took the reins and moved his racer to the starting line there was always a very loud response from the spectators who universally respected the champion.

The course length for the horse races was one quarter of a mile and there were five heats to each race. The winner was the horse winning the best three out of five. These events were sponsored by the Newfoundland Horseman's Association. In 1949, the Association sponsored the events to raise funds for Memorial Stadium Building Fund. No dogs were permitted in the area because of concern they might frighten the horses or interfere with them during the races. A sound truck was present to play music and after the races it supplied music for general skating on the Pond.

Joey Judge had two wins and two second places plus several third place spots. Mcdonald Gratton tied him with the same record and the judges called for a "Who Shall." This was a special race to decide the best racer for the day. However, we were all disappointed when it was announced that there would be no 'Who shall' that day because one of the horses was not available. I knew the champion in my mind that day was Joey Judge.

On the day we attended the horse racing, an unusual accident took place. A horse named 'Sulley,' driven by Eddie Vincent and owned by Warrick Marshall, crossed the line in first place in the Pacers Race. After crossing the line, the shaft of the gig broke and Vincent was tossed arse over kettle across the ice. The horse, after falling, quickly got to its feet and panicked. She took off across the pond to the Star Boat House, then up the road towards King's Bridge.

We were very amused at the spectacle. Many people were trying to stop the runaway horse but to no avail. She left a trail of heroic men in the snow banks along the way. She finally stopped on her own in front of Tobin's Store on King's Bridge Road. Fortunately, there were no serious injuries.

Other horses involved in these races included Mcdonald Gratton owned by R. Lester and driven by Harry Bugden, and Hush Money owned by Joey Judge. Skipper Walsh's horse Moses H. was one of the top race horses of that era, however he was not racing that day.

Wintertime involved a variety of exciting outdoor activities, but it was always nice to get indoors and warm up once the fun was over. The most popular place in any house in wintertime was the kitchen and the most sought after spot was in front of the old coal and wood stove. The kitchen stove provided the heat for the house. Actually, the kitchen door in winter was always kept closed to keep the heat in that area. For the most part the rest of the house remained unheated. Some people had hall coal stoves which were effective in warming other parts of the house as well. On cold winter nights family and visitors would congregate in the kitchen all vying for a place close to the warmth of the coal stove. After a few hours sliding or skating outside it was always pleasant to enjoy the warmth of a heated kitchen and a good cup of hot chocolate or hot tea.

Visiting the homes of friends you would see a variety of coal stoves. There was the coal range which was modernistic in appearance with its temperature gauge and white enamel, and silver metallic borders. There were as many models of the range as there were stores that sold them. One I remember well was the Maid of Avalon. Then there was the old Ideal Cook type stove which by the year 1950 was on its way out. these were black metal stoves with a grate through which you could watch the fire burn. Very few people had toasters and most made toast by placing a fork in a piece of bread and laying the bread against the grate. When smoke began to rise from the bread, you would take it away and turn the bread upside down and then replace it until it again smoked. At this point you had your toast. It was a cumbersome way to make toast but it did have a distinctive flavour that modern day toasters could never replicate. Toasting home-made bread often added to the warmth of the kitchen in winter.

These stoves required wood and coal on a daily basis. Wood, or splits, were used to start the fire. Dry splits wrapped in newspaper were placed into the stove with several lumps of coal on top. The burning paper would ignite the splits and flaming splits would in turn ignite the coal. Family members took turns shovelling coal into the stove. Before going to bed on a cold winter's night parents would 'bank down,' the fire. This was done by putting a shovel full of ash's over the burning fire. This would cause the fire to smoulder throughout the night and make it easier to get a good fire going in the morning. It also provided some heat throughout the night.

We had electrical blackouts in those days as we do now, but they did not present the calamity and problems for householders as is the case today. The major inconvenience in a winter blackout is the loss of heat, but in those days the majority of homes were heated by wood and coal stoves. These would function well with or without a blackout. If a family ran short of fuel they could provide heat by burning wood and all sorts of household garbage.

I recall passing one blackout with my brother sitting at our kitchen table and making candles from the burning wax of candles in use. We first made a wick by dipping a piece of string in melted wax and allowing it to harden. Then we would take the melted candle wax when it was partially hardened and roll it around the wick. They were rather crude candles but they served the purpose well,and they entertained us for hours.

During one major blackout a family living in the top flat of a three story house on Flower Hill had a harrowing experience that left an impression on neighbours for decades. The transformer on one of the poles exploded and the wire appeared to be burning with its flame moving like a burning fuse towards the house. George, the father of two children, and prone to displays of bravado, was the first in the family to notice the advancing threat.

He immediately took control of the situation. Confidently, George grabbed several bed sheets and tied them together. He then grabbed a chair and smashed open the window so he could use the sheets as an escape route. He shouted orders to his wife to get the kids out first but when he turned around there was no one but himself left in the flat. As a matter of fact, there was no one but George left in the house. Everyone else had evacuated over the stairs and out the front door. George's wife Rita had grabbed their children and went down over the three flights of stairs and out the front door thinking George was following behind her.

George had the window broken and the sheets hanging out blowing in the wind when Rita angrily shouted, "What's wrong with the front door, ya bloody fool!" The wire-fire fizzled out, but not the memories of George's embarrassment. He was the object of so much ribbing from neighbourhood men at the popular Gosse's Tavern that he had to give up going to Gosse's.

Christmas Spirit

A unity of spirit brings people together at Christmas time in a way that no other event can achieve. Most people's thoughts are directed towards Christmas and the celebration of that most joyous and wonderful of all seasons.

Children needed no calendar to be aware that Christmas was drawing near. We were exposed to all sorts of indicators that something special was happening. There were more visits to the downtown stores. There were no shopping centres or malls in those days: Water Street had it all. There were clothing stores, shoe stores, furniture stores, paint and paper shops, large department stores with a variety of commodities, meat markets, fruit stores, restaurants and even gypsy fortune tellers. Auto traffic was not a major problem but pedestrian traffic was always heavy. Whole families carrying bags of goods made their way from Water Street, up over the hills to their homes in downtown St. John's.

The larger department stores featured a Christmas toyland which opened about a month before Christmas, and closed just after that blessed event. Bowring Brothers, Ayre's Ltd., and The Royal Stores all redesigned sections of their huge stores which they converted into a Toyland. Children would line up to visit these magical wonderlands, then rush home to tell their parents about some wonderful gift that could be purchased there. The parents' response was always the same, "You might get what you want if you stay good until Christmas." There was the added warning that if you were bad, "Santa will leave a lump of coal for you."

In those times children were told that Santa entered the house by coming down the chimney. Every home had a chimney; it was a necessity in those days of coal and wood as heating fuel. It was important that little children go to bed early on Christmas Eve or Santa wouldn't come. And of course, before going to bed you had to leave something for Santa. A piece of Christmas Cake and a glass of syrup was the bait to get Santa into the house.

An essential part of the season on Water Street was the Christmas Raffle. Several raffles operated from various locations along the Street. The most popular was the Mount Cashel Raffle, but there were others. Crowds were beckoned into the raffle by the sound of the clanging of a bell rung by a young boy wrapped in warm winter clothing. When the temperatures dropped to chill the winter's night and the flakes of snow trickled slowly down coating every-thing—buildings, streets and even people—in winter white, the interior of a raffle had a warm and cosy appeal to the passerby. The raffles were always crowded with people hoping to win one of the many turkeys or hams for Christmas dinner. Mount Cashel always had several live turkeys in the window to attract the interest of those on the outside. The build up of excitement on Water Street did not go unnoticed by us. Gangs of children mixed with the nightly crowds on Water Street competing for a spot in front of the many department store windows to view the splendid Christmas displays and decorations. The raffle bells, sleigh bells of the horse and wagons passing by, the crunch of snow beneath our feet and the happy, friendly spirit outwardly shown by everyone, gave the season a sprinkling of magic.

Water Street, however, was not the only source of Christmas purchasing for the city population. There was catalogue shopping from Eaton's and Simpson-Sears. These featured pages and pages of all sorts of gift ideas. Glancing through the catalogue was often enough to ignite the Christmas spirit. There were the arrays of all sorts of Christmas candies, chocolates and fruit cakes. These items were packed into an appealing decorated box or tin can, and made splendid Christmas gifts. Marvellous toys, appliances and winter clothing were all set out for the catalogue shopper to choose from.

Yet, buying by catalogue had its problems. You had to get your order in long before Christmas to assure its delivery in time for the great holiday. I remember one Christmas which was ruined because Simpsons failed to deliver in time for Santa. I was five years old and my brother Maurice was eight. I was still certain that Santa was real and thought my brother was risking getting a lump of coal in his stocking by suggesting that Santa did not exist. My mother had ordered gifts from Simpsons and we both knew what Santa Claus was going to bring. My brother was keen on a basketball set with a regulation size ball and net. I couldn't wait to get my hands on a toy pool table. We both sat down many nights looking at the catalogue pictures of our desired gifts, and imagining how much fun we were going to have on Christmas Day. That was the Christmas I learned the truth about Santa Claus.

When Christmas Eve arrived my mother was obviously upset. All week she had been pestering Simpsons about the delivery date of her order. Christmas Eve arrived and she walked down to the Simpson Store on Water Street hoping to pick up her order. The clerk did a lot of checking and rechecking before expressing her regrets that the parcel had not arrived as promised. The clerk apologized but promised that the order would definitely be in the store the day after Boxing Day.

My mother had no choice but to purchase other gifts. It was Christmas Eve and no time was left. That Christmas Eve was unlike any other I had experienced. My father, who worked on the passenger ship, *Fort Amherst*, was out to sea and would not be home for Christmas. And now, the gifts we had written Santa for were not coming. I could sense the disappointment and sadness my mother was feeling. She decided it was time to tell us the truth about Christmas. It was shattering for me but my older brother took it in stride. He already knew what every grown up knew about Santa Claus. Somehow, over the years I have totally forgotten the substitute gifts but I remember with clarity the little pool table I dreamed about. It did come after Christmas, but Christmas was never the same.

Getting ready for Christmas was a ritual in every city household. Getting ready meant laying new canvas on the kitchen floor at least, new wallpaper, and a new oil cloth for the kitchen table. An oil cloth was a table covering which usually lasted from one Christmas to the next. There was always a wide assortment of colours and patterns to choose from. These table cloths had a distinctive aroma and the minute you went into a house and picked up that scent you knew instantly that there was a new table cloth there.

Wallpapering the house and laying canvas was another sign that we were into the Christmas season. Wallpapering was an art. A special paste of flour and water had to be mixed and this glue kept the paper stuck to the wall. On the evenings when household jobs like these were being done, we were able to stay out later at night. For this reason we loved to see canvas and wallpaper being delivered to our home. It also defined more clearly a special time of year, a very special season.

One needed a great deal of patience and skill to hang wall paper. Several rolls would be needed to do each room, and each roll had to be lined up to match the other. Many a household dispute erupted during the wallpapering of a room. I remember when houses in the area were being torn down in the mid 1950s noticing the layer upon layer of wallpaper on kitchen and bedroom walls. I know you can tell the age of a tree by the number of rings; perhaps you could tell how many Christmases were celebrated in a house by the layers of wallpaper. Each layer told a story.

When the wallpapering was done, a border was installed near the ceiling or in the middle of the wall. A great deal of study accompanied the selection of just the right pattern of wall paper and matching border.

When the papering was done, the canvas laid and the ceilings painted (white), all that remained to complete the Christmas preparations was the tree and its decorations.

The exterior signs of Christmas were not as common as they are today. The Water Street stores decorated their windows, but private homes did not display outside lights or trees. The corner grocery store was decorated with red and green bunting and crepe Christmas bells hanging from the centre of the store. A common display in the neighbourhood stores was the lifesize Santa Claus, advertising some product like Coke or Pepsi. However, the interior of houses glistened and sparkled with tinsel decorations and lights. There was no such thing as an artificial Christmas tree—everyone had the real thing. Some cut their own but most people purchased them from vendors all over the City. Some vendors even went door to door peddling the trees which sold for one dollar.

In my home the Christmas tree was not purchased until Christmas Eve. The practice of leaving the tree until Christmas Eve was very common and in keeping with observing the twelve day Christmas season. I remember my father with hammer and nail and the help of Mike or Harry Murphy positioning the tree in the corner of our kitchen. While he got the tree set up my mother was busy cleaning and dressing the turkey and while she had already baked her dark and light Christmas cakes weeks before, she always made a Chocolate Cake on Christmas Eve. (In those days people called round cakes pies).

My brother and I would be persuaded to go to bed at 8 p.m. with the warning that if Santa Claus came to the house and we were still up he would not come inside. Although we went to bed early, it was a real challenge to go to sleep. Friends and neighbours dropped in throughout the night and we could hear the singing of Christmas songs. This added to the excitement of Christmas Eve. Harry and Mary Murphy, who lived in the flat above ours, were regular visitors on Christmas Eve and inevitably Mary would sing "Christmas in Kilarney."

Most parents would have been horrified if everything had not been ready before Christmas Eve. But, Christmas Eve was only the start of Christmas for us. We went to bed with everything up in slings, as we used to say to describe things being left undone. Very early in the morning my brother and I would walk into the kitchen still wiping the sleep from our eyes. Most trees were erected in the kitchen area. Because of the overcrowding in houses many did not have a living room, or "parlour" as they were then called.

All we needed to prove that Christmas was magical and Santa Claus was real was there before us. The stark, green-bowed tree of the night before was now a tinkling masterpiece of tinsel, coloured ornaments of every size, wrapped in red and green garland, icicles, angel hair, glowing tree lights and adorned on top with a large brightly-lit star. (Holy Cross School had an annual fall fair known as the Pantry Shelf. I remember in 1951 experiencing delight in winning a tree top angel at one of these fairs. This angel adorned our Christmas tree up until the time my own son Maurice was born in 1969.)

We would always look to the kitchen table for confirmation that Santa had been here. Before we went to bed on Christmas Eve my brother and I would be asked to prepare a lunch for Santa and leave it on the kitchen table. We prepared a glass of Stafford's Strawberry syrup and a plate of light and dark Christmas cake and an assortment of cookies. The empty glass and the empty plate was Santa's signature for us. There was no doubt left. He had been here. Then our eyes would settle beneath the tree which was like a little toyland. Gifts were simple and inexpensive in those days. Cars, trucks, cowboy guns with holsters for boys; dolls, cribs and carriages for girls.

Every house had a Christmas wreath in each window. These were made of red cellophane or plastic. As we became more modern, the electrically lighted wreath with the candle in the centre became popular. However, outdoor electric displays, or displays of any sort, were confined to Government buildings and Department stores.

While the exterior displays of Christmas so common today were not part of our lives then, there seemed to be more Christmas activity inside the homes. For weeks before Christmas, mothers would busy themselves baking goods for the Christmas season. Fruit and cherry cakes were made early and stored until Christmas Eve. Then there would be an assortment of shortbreads, and other cakes and buns.

Although mummering is talked and written about today

as though it was a great Newfoundland Christmas tradition I never saw or even heard mention of a mummer or of mummering during the 1940s and 1950s. As a matter of fact it was not until 1972 I became aware that there had been a Newfoundland mummering tradition in the 19th century. Yet, even without the mummers or tales of mummers Christmas was always memorable. There were twelve days of Christmas, actually thirteen days from December 25th to old Christmas Day on January 6th.

Christmas was a time for visiting. People made the rounds of homes in the neighbourhood. Children especially delighted in those visits. They would gather together in groups and go knocking on doors. "Can we come in and see your Christmas tree?" they would ask of whoever answered the door. There was always a welcome response. After all it was a long-standing custom and an opportunity to share the Christmas spirit. The invitation inside meant a treat for the children. The usual fare for these visits included orange, raspberry and strawberry syrups; an assortment of home baked Christmas fruit cakes; shortbreads and other cookies and of course a variety of Christmas candy. In return for being invited into a home, children would be asked to entertain. This usually involved the group singing a Christmas carol or two before departing for the next house and more treats. Needless to say there was much over-indulging and a great deal of merriment.

Adults of course would drop in on neighbours to wish the best for the season and would be treated to home made wines, and home brews, in addition to the alcoholic beverages purchased at the liquor store and stored for the occasion. There was always someone who would wear out their welcome by staying too long, or partaking in excess of what the host had to offer. In the odd case where a fight threatened to erupt there was the Black Mariah to drag away the unwelcome guest to the city lock-up.

A family I remember well for their Christmas spirit was the family of Harry and Mary Murphy, our neighbours on Flower Hill. The Murphys had ten children and they would begin preparations weeks before Christmas. Harry and Mary had lots of home baked treats, as well as brews of gin, rum and wine. They were the only family I ever encountered that celebrated each of the twelve nights of Christmas. To do that one needed a good supply of spirits.

Liquor was not easy to obtain. It could only be purchased from the Board of Liquor stores and then only if you had a liquor book which permitted you to buy two bottles per week. Home brews and home made wines were quite common as a way to supplement the Government liquor ration. I don't think anyone could match Harry or Mary in making home brews. They could make brews out of all sorts of things. Harry was especially known for his dogberry and blueberry wines, while Mary excelled at making Gin.

I recall one Christmas when Harry and Mary had brewed a batch of blueberry wine for the holiday celebrations. Mary, only too aware of Harry's habit of over-sampling the product, put the entire batch under the kitchen cupboard and put a padlock on it. Anyone with experience in making a brew know only too well the possibility of exploding bottles.

On this occasion, Mary left the house to do some downtown shopping. She returned home several hours later. The house reeked of alcohol, blueberry wine to be exact; and it looked like the brew had spilled over the floor. Harry was resting on the kitchen couch singing, "It's a Long Way to Tipperary," his favourite song when he had had a few drinks. He was quick to offer an explanation to Mary. "The brew exploded. I couldn't get into the cupboard because you didn't

leave me the key. I think we lost it all by the look of things."
Harry was able to keep a straight, serious face when explaining the mishap. But Mary was not easily fooled. She noticed the broom on the floor by the cupboard, and several overturned small glasses.

From this evidence she concluded, Harry had used the broom handle to shove into a small opening in the cupboard and smashed the brew bottles. She speculated that he then scooped up the alcohol spurting out through the crevices with the glasses until he got his fill of the brew. Harry vehemently denied it, assuring her he would never do such a thing. He never did explain to Mary's satisfaction where he had gotten the alcohol to get drunk that day. Harry maintained his innocence for years after, and argued that he was not at all drunk. He explained he just had the flu and it had thrown him off a little. What really happened to the brew is still a mystery debated every Christmas when the Murphy family gathers to celebrate as they have done for several generations. The ladies are certain that Mary was right and Harry had gotten into the brew. The men however, insist Harry was telling the truth.

Concealing the home brew from Harry was always a challenge to Mary. On another occasion she had made some very fine home brewed Gin. She knew better than to hide it in the cupboard with the padlock a second time. A locked cupboard would be the first place Harry would seek out. This time, Mary went to the attic and hid the Gin in the bottom of an old trunk filled with linen and clothing items.

Confident that she had outwitted Harry, Mary set out to do some Water Street shopping. Several hours passed before she returned home. As she approached her front door on Flower Hill, she could hear once again the strains of, "It's a Long Way to Tipperary." Mary crossed her fingers and whispered a short prayer, pleading that it wasn't her Gin he had been drinking. Perhaps, a friend had dropped in with a drink?. Mary wondered. Her pace quickened and with each step and each musical note coming from her kitchen, her blood pressure went up a point. Before Harry could say anything, Mary demanded to know if he had been dipping into her Gin. Harry replied indignantly, "I did not have a drink. I don't even know where you hid the stuff." Mary rushed up over the stairs to the attic to inspect the old trunk. She was absolutely certain she would find empty or broken bottles. But, to her surprise, the bottles were all intact and filled as she had left them.

She now felt guilty that she had wrongfully accused Harry. She returned to the kitchen in a more pleasant spirit and prepared supper for Harry and the children. A couple of weeks later she brought the Gin from the attic for Christmas Eve visitors. When Harry viewed the Gin bottles on the table he grabbed his coat and said he had to go out on a message and would be back in fifteen minutes. Soon after Frank (Teeney) Murphy, Harry's son opened a bottle of gin and poured everyone a drink. It was a memorable Christmas Eve at the Murphy household. The Gin had somehow turned into pure water. Mary knew that Harry had outwitted her. Replacing the Gin with water didn't take Harry long, but it was a long while before Mary spoke to him after that.

Making a brew had its risks. If the bottles didn't explode, other unforseen circumstances could destroy it. Jimmy Hearn had to sacrifice an entire brew on one occasion in order to save his house.

Jimmy had stored a brew in the basement of his Flower Hill home, anticipating it would be ready for the Christmas season. Several days before Christmas a cold spell dropped temperatures below freezing.

When the frost caused the pipes in the basement to freeze, Jimmy took a blow torch to the area in an effort to thaw them out. During the process calamity struck. The heat from the torch caught fire to the house and Jimmy and his son-in-law Dave King had to move fast to prevent the flames from spreading.

A quick glance around determined that the only means off fighting the fire was the capped brew. They began popping open the bottles one by one and pouring the beer over the flames until they finally doused the fire. By that time, there was not a drop of beer left. But they saved the house and possibly prevented a greater tragedy.

(The only similar event to this that I am aware of took place at the turn of the century on Pleasant Street. In that incident a housewife used a vat of Spruce Beer being saved for the Regatta, to douse a fire in her house. That episode made the local newspapers.)

Harry and Mary Murphy's daughter Beth pitched in one Christmas to help her mother with the Christmas baking. Mary gave her the recipe for her delicious dark fruitcake and Beth set out to mix the ingredients. Mary, meanwhile was busy with other household duties preparing for Christmas Day. Beth was progressing well with her mothers recipe until she came to "mix in two eggs." Beth stopped, thought for awhile then called her mother to the kitchen. She asked, "Mom, I got to put two eggs in this . . . do I fry em or boil em ?" Mary grabbed Beth by the arm and ordered her out of the kitchen. She then muttered to Harry, "That Beth is as stunned as me arse."

Even years later when Beth was married and rearing her own family Harry frequently taunted her about her cooking. One Christmas Harry and Mary had Christmas dinner with Beth and her family at their home on Codner's Lane. Beth went through a lot of trouble to prepare the dinner and felt quite proud of her effort. When Harry finished eating Beth eagerly asked how he had enjoyed the meal. Harry with a contemplative look commented, "It was a dinner fit for a King." Then with his impish grin he added, "Here King . . . here King . . . here b'y." Beth had a small rusty coloured terrier named King.

One Christmas season Mary Murphy received word that a cousin of hers, who was a Presentation Nun, was to visit the City and would be dropping in for a visit. She quickly laid down the law to Harry. Harry had a great sense of humour and Mary was concerned that he might embarrass her in front of the nun. On the day of the visit Mary prepared a home cooked traditional meal of pork and cabbage with a steamed blueberry pudding for desert. She had one bottle of blueberry wine left from her Christmas supply and knew her cousin loved a glass of this Newfoundland beverage. On the day of the visit Mary told Harry that he was not to have anything to drink. She told him in no uncertain terms that when time came to distribute the wine he was to accept only one drink and not dare venture to have another.

Mary Murphy's Christmas Party: Mary and Harry Murphy stepping it out at a Christmas party in their home.

Finally, the nun arrived at the door with a sister nun and they were welcomed into the Murphy home. The nuns thoroughly enjoyed the dinner and the pudding. Following the meal Mary opened the wine and poured a drink for the two nuns then one for herself. As she poured Harry's she looked at him with an expression that said . . . one drink and only one drink. Harry graciously accepted the drink then proposed a toast to the health of the visiting sisters.

While the nuns and Mary conversed Harry's attention focused on the half bottle of wine left on the table. He wondered if he could get away with pouring another drink. The topic of conversation turned to religious beliefs. The good sister was lamenting the fact that many people were losing their faith and expressed the feeling that it was important to maintain your beliefs throughout life. Unexpectedly she turned to Harry and asked if he agreed. With one eye on the bottle and the other on the nun, Harry answered, "Yes sister, I believe everyone should believe in something. And right now, I believe I'll have another drink."

Mary knew she was outsmarted again. She barely controlled her anger until the good nuns had departed then she grabbed the remainder of the wine which Harry was about to claim and poured it down the sink.

Some years later I played a practical joke on Mary which neither of us ever forgot. It happened during the Christmas season. I placed a handkerchief over my telephone receiver to disguise my voice and I called Mary. I told her I was a linesman with the Avalon Telephone Company and I was up on the poles outside repairing damaged lines in the area. I then warned her that she was not to use or answer the telephone for the next fifteen minutes. I explained that the lines I was working on were live and if she picked up the receiver I could receive a severe electric shock or even worse, be electrocuted. She assured me of her cooperation.

As soon as she hung up the phone I dialled her number. It rang, and rang and rang. Finally, she reluctantly picked up the receiver. When she did, I screamed into my phone,"Ahhhhhhhhhhhhhhhh!" I could hear her shout,

"Good Jesus Alex, I think I killed him." I was laughing so hard that I found it difficult to explain to her but she quickly recognized my voice. "If I had my hands around your throat right now, you wouldn't be laughing," she reacted angrily. An hour later I was at her front door with a bottle of Cold Duck Wine and a box of Pot-o-Gold chocolates to wish her a Merry Christmas. By that time she had cooled down, and was laughing at the joke herself. Mary had a great sense of humour and loved fun, especially at Christmas time.

Midnight mass was another part of the Christmas celebrations. I was just nine years old when I attended my first midnight mass. There was always discussion among family and neighbours on Christmas Eve as to who was or was not going to midnight mass. I had attended the weekly children's mass at St. Patrick's Church, but the idea of the Christmas midnight mass had a mystic appeal to me. I was sure it had to be something different and wonderful to experience. My father was planning on taking my twelve-year-old brother Maurice to midnight mass at the Basilica. This was even more intriguing for me because I rarely got to see the inside of the Basilica. My parents tried to reason with me that midnight mass was not for children, especially little boys. I argued that if Maurice could go I should be able to go. I nagged and nagged my father until he gave in and agreed to take me. With me going, my mother had no reason to stay home so we went as a family.

It was not a white Christmas. We had four consecutive days of drizzle and rain which diminished the Christmas spirit. But once inside the huge Basilica the mood instantly changed. There was the magnificent Nativity Crib and the boughs which surrounded it produced one of the common smells associated with Christmas, the Christmas tree scent. The church was filled to capacity with standing room only.

People were dressed in their Sunday best and the altar area was adorned with beautiful flowers and glowing candles. At precisely midnight the Archbishop, clad in his splendid and colourful attire, was escorted to the altar by a procession of 130 altar boys in their attractive red and white tunics. At the same time an eighty member choir began singing "O Holy Night." The choir master that night was Basil Hutton and Barbara Buckley was the organist. My father lifted me onto the pew to get a better view of the procession. I was enthralled by the ceremony until the Archbishop went to the pulpit to talk . . . and he talked . . . and he talked . . . and he talked. "Good Lord," I said to myself, "is he ever going to stop?" It seemed there would be no end to it.

It was then I understood my parents' strong efforts to discourage me from going to midnight mass. I quickly tired, and dozed off into a deep sleep. I was awakened by a nudge from my father beckoning me to follow him. Everyone was leaving the church. Although, I slept through most of the mass I was impressed with what I had witnessed and it left me with a nice warm Christmas feeling. That midnight mass of 1952 was the only Christmas mass that I remember ever attending with my entire family. My father passed away two years later and my brother was killed in an automobile accident nine years later.

Snow storms in the 1950s seemed to be a lot more severe than those of today. I remember climbing a snow bank at the corner of Flower Hill and Central Street and actually touching the top of a light pole. Certainly, there are many old pictures which depict such incredible scenes of pole-high snow banks around St. John's at that time. It was following one such storm a few days before Christmas in 1953 or 1954 that the following incident took place.

Tony Jesseau, well known in sporting circles in St. John's

for several decades, was sent by his mother to Glasco's Butcher Shop on Brazil Square to pick up a turkey for Christmas dinner. The Jesseau family lived on John Street just a short distance from the butcher shop. Mrs. Jesseau always ordered a fresh turkey from Bob Glasco and had it picked up the day before Christmas Eve.

Tony, accompanied by his friend Bottles Janes had to battle high snow drifts along the street to get to the butcher shop. With the turkey under his arm he and Bottles set out to bring it home.

They climbed to the top of the snow bank which ran from the bottom to Stack's Store at the top of Brazil Square. Unknown to them some children had carved out a snow cave at one point in the bank of snow. When Tony and Bottles were directly over it, the snow gave way and they fell crashing into the cavity with the snow piling in on top of them. They managed to claw their way out of the snow but in the process lost the turkey.

It took the two young boys almost two hours of hard work shovelling snow before they found the lost turkey. Tony later recalled it seemed like they had to shovel half Brazil Square to uncover the buried turkey. It was a Christmas Tony and Bottles never forgot. This may have happened the same year the people of Hagerty Street and John Street did their own snow clearing after a severe winter storm that paralysed the City for several days. Householders on these streets banded together and, using shovels, cleared their own streets rather than wait for the overburdened city snow clearers to do the job.

A house party to celebrate New Year's Eve and to welcome in the New Year was very much a part of most downtown households in the 1950s. As midnight approached and the countdown began, revellers prepared to move their party

L-R: *Mary Murphy, son Frank and husband Harry.*

outdoors. They put on sweaters, coats or wrapped in blankets then grabbed anything available in the house which had potential as a noisemaker. Most often these included kitchen items like pots, pans, and kettles. They used spoons, forks and knives as drum sticks to pound on the kitchen utensils. Some even had guns ready to fire at midnight.

With party goers pouring into the streets the celebrations became a neighbourhood party. On Flower Hill there on the streets counting down to midnight were the Murphys, the Cranshaws, the Fardys, the Abbotts, the Constantines, the Crottys, the Smiths, the Bartletts, the Hickeys, the Malones, the McDonalds, the Nobles, the Whelans, the Fowlers, the Williams, the Fitzgeralds, the Hearns, the Sears, the Ryans, the Hanames, the Prowses, the Leonards, the Hipditchs, the Butlers, the Warrens, the Andrews, the Walshs, and the Meaneys. Even elderly couples who were not having a party ventured outside to join in the spirit of the event.

When the countdown started everyone joined in 10 - 9 - 8 - 7 - 6 - 5 - 4 - 3 - 2 - 1 -. . . then as the clanging and banging of the improvised noisemakers permeated the night air the whole City came alive. Church bells rang out, the ships in port sounded their whistles and rang their bells, all combining with the neighbourhood pandemonium to give a joyous welcome to the New Year. People joined in singing Auld Lang Syne and embraced and kissed each other as they mingled to wish each other a Happy New Year.

Royal Aerated Water Co. Ltd. manufacturers of Royal Beverages were located on Barter's Hill near New Gower Street.

Rawlins Cross: Photo taken around 1948 just before street cars were taken of city streets. It shows a scene at Rawlins Cross. The police officer controlled traffic lights from the booth to the right.

After Frank Murphy (son of Harry and Mary Murphy) married Jean Baird of New Gower Street they moved to Greenwood, Nova Scotia where they set up a small bakery. On the first New Year's Eve in Greenwood, they were celebrating at home alone and lamenting the happy and noisy New Year's Eve celebrations in neighbourhoods back home. Frank, decided that they would ring in the New Year as they had always done. They grabbed some pots and pans and went out into the street pounding on them and shouting Happy New Year. Frank and Jean had expected the street to be filled with people ringing in the New Year, but it wasn't. Two neighbours challenged Frank to a fight and an elderly lady living across the street telephoned Frank and threatened to call the police or have him committed if he didn't stop making noise. Frank and Jean realized then that not everyone celebrated the New Year in the same way as the good people of Flower Hill. After telephoning relatives in St. John's to wish them a Happy New year Frank and Jean retired for the night. The experience left them homesick and looking forward to the day when they would return to live in St. John's.

Old Time Wakes

A morbid pall descended over the neighbourhood when anyone passed away, or was "promoted to glory" as the Salvation Army say. All homes had window blinds; usually of green colour which in the day time were wound around a roller board that fitted across the window top. Normally, as darkness approached these blinds were pulled down to prevent the public from seeing into the home. When someone passed away in a house the curtains were pulled to and the blinds on all front windows in the house of the deceased would be completely pulled down. The blinds would remain in that position until the funeral was over. Neighbours would show their respect for the deceased by pulling their blinds down only half way.

After a man's funeral, his widow continued to show she was in mourning by wearing black clothing for a year. When neighbours referred to a widow they rarely mentioned her first name, or even Mrs. So-and-so. It was, "The widow Murphy is doing very well," or "the widow Snow is over her mourning." Only when she remarried would the reference 'widow' be dropped.

It was not a custom for funeral homes to wake the dead. The undertaker removed the body, prepared it for burial and placed it in a coffin—usually built at the undertakers—but the body was returned home for the wake. The undertakers experienced frequent problems in getting the coffins into and out the homes. First they would manoeuvre the coffin upright to get into the hallway. Then there would be twists and turns until finally they managed to get it to the wake room, a kitchen, bedroom or living room, depending what was available. It was not at all unusual to see them remove doors or extract the coffin from a window. A Barter's Hill man who weighed over 300 pounds passed away in a second story bedroom. They couldn't get him out through the narrow hallways so they attempted to remove him through a bedroom window. This also proved to be impossible. There were two separate windows in the bedroom. When all else failed they had to cut through the wall dividing the window and remove the body using pulleys through the large opening created.

There were more undertakers than we have today. There was Oake's on Quidi Vidi Road; Carnell's on Cochrane Street; Jimmy Martin—which became Caul's—on the corner of New Gower Street and Lime Street; Wall's on Duckworth Street and Murphy's on Bambrick Street. All funeral homes had horse-drawn funeral carriages which carried the casket to the church for services and then the cemetery.

The wakes took place in the home where the remains were kept for two nights and burial took place on the third day. Friends of the family would clear a suitable room in the home to wake the deceased. Embalming methods were not as advanced as today. The mortician placed white cotton balls in both nostrils of the corpse to prevent the odour emanating from the inside of the deceased person. The tradition of burying people in a burial habit was on its way out by the 1950s. A burial habit was a long hooded gown similar to the habits worn by Monks. There was always someone in a neighbourhood who made and sold these habits. People often purchased them and kept them stored in the home until needed. The last such habit I recall seeing was at the funeral of Harry Carew in 1950. Harry was a decorated veteran of World War Two and operated a tug at Dunkirk which helped evacuate allied troops during that historic battle. Harry was waked in the upstairs living room of his home on Springdale Street. His burial habit was brown silk with a crest of the Sacred Heart sewn onto it.

Neighbours would lend chairs to be used for those paying their last respect. There was no set time to visit and pay last respects; the home received visitors around the clock, and nobody in the family got any rest, apart from the odd catnap. Neighbours brought food to the family of the deceased. At Catholic wakes there was always the rosary followed by a cup of tea. There were many cups of tea throughout the wake.

With a crowd gathered in a small space for so many hours it was inevitable that wakes became a source of much humour. Everyone had a funny story to tell. Sometimes there would be loud outbursts of laughter, but this meant no disrespect for the dead. It was a practice that eased the pain of the mourning family.

There is a story told of a Mr. Narcozie who owned a store on New Gower Street but lived on Cabot Street. During the early hours of the morning on the first night of the wake pranksters sat Narcozie up in his coffin and left him there to startle mourners dropping in throughout the night. My cousin Don Carew and I witnessed another startling occurrence during the wake of an aunt who had passed away at a youthful age. We were about five or six years old at the time. The coffin was placed in the downstairs kitchen of my grandmother's home on Barter's Hill as it was impossible to get the coffin up over the narrow stairway to a second floor living room. At one point during the wake everyone moved to the upstairs living room, leaving the coffin unattended in the kitchen.

Don and I were sitting on the bottom step of the stairway and had an unobstructed view of the coffin. An old lady dressed in black and wearing a black laced shawl over her head came in and stood over the coffin. She placed her hands into the coffin and it appeared to us that she was pulling at something. She then leaned in over and placed her head down into the coffin. This really aroused our curiosity.

Quietly, so as not to draw attention to ourselves we stood up on the stairway and peeked into the coffin. The old lady was trying to remove the ring from my aunt's finger using her teeth. When we realized what was happening we broke into laughter. She turned quickly towards us with a surprised but scornful look and shook her fist at us. We ran upstairs and hid near a window at the end of the hallway. We could hear the creaking of the stairway as the old lady made her way up. We thought for sure she was coming after us. But when she got to the living room door she went in and sat down with the other mourners.

It was at 19 Barter's Hill (Centre house) where Jack Fitzgerald witnessed an attempt to steal from the coffin of a deceased person.

We were too scared to tell anyone that night of what we had witnessed. I recall it was sometime after the funeral that we told other family members. If anything was ever done about it we were never told.

When the time came to remove the casket from the home,

everyone except the women and the pall bearers would go outside and form a procession line behind the horse-drawn hearse. Only males could participate in the procession. The ladies remained in the home. Relatives of the deceased wore black: The men wore black suits, white shirts and black ties; the women wore black dresses and/or sweaters. Others attending the funeral wore black neckties.

The pall bearers removed the coffin and placed it on the hearse. The funeral director, dressed in black with a black top hat, would walk in front of the hearse and the procession would make its way through the streets to the neighbourhood church for the funeral service. After the service the procession would move through the streets of St. John's to the appropriate cemetery. People along the way would stop; Catholics blessed themselves and bowed their heads; others bowed their heads or placed their right hand over their heart. Gentlemen always removed their hats. Passing cars or horse drawn vehicles also stopped until the procession passed.

It was not unusual to see Silly Willy, one of the town characters, step to the front of a funeral procession and pretend to lead it right to the church or graveyard. Silly Willy was known by everyone and freely wandered the town. Whenever he emerged from a crowd to lead a funeral procession it only provided a little amusement for the mourners. Willy always dressed in a long black overcoat and a salt and pepper hat. His trademark was his runny nose.

An amusing incident occurred at my father's funeral in 1954. I was just eleven years old at the time and my brother Maurice was fourteen. As tradition demanded we led the funeral procession. The coffin was removed by six pall bearers from the house and placed on a horse-drawn carriage. The funeral director, dressed in black and wearing a top hat, led the horse while my brother and I led the procession. The procession went from Charlton Street to St. Patrick's Church for services at 3 p.m. After funeral service the procession moved up Patrick Street and east along Hamilton Avenue and New Gower Street towards Mount Carmel Cemetery. Just after passing Queen Street the incident occurred which surprised and startled Maurice and me. I overheard Kev Yetman ask my Uncle Frank if he wanted to bet on it. I had no idea as to what they were betting on.

As the procession approached Mammy Gosse's Tavern the horse turned from the road to pull in alongside the Tavern. The sudden change caused some temporary confusion but the funeral director quickly directed the horse back onto the street. The incident sparked some laughter among the mourners and we soon learned that the horse had pulled into Gosse's out of habit. It was only then that it became clear that Kev Yetman knew that the funeral director was a regular patron of the tavern and that the horse was very accustomed to turning in at that spot. He was willing to bet it would happen again that day.

On an earlier occasion one funeral made newspaper reports. Jimmy Martin, funeral director of J.T. Martins, had hired a reformed alcoholic to drive the hearse. It was the hottest summer day in years when the procession left St. Patrick's Church in the west end for Mount Carmel cemetery in the east end. The driver's thoughts turned to the refreshing memories of a cold beer. The temptation grew as the procession moved along. At Gosse's the driver decided he was going to have a few beers come hell or high water. The procession was not moving along fast enough for him so he jiggled the reins to make the horse move faster. The men walking behind the hearse increased their pace to keep up. Near Hotel Newfoundland, the driver was so anxious that he struck the horse with the whip and once again the speed increased. Once again those in the funeral procession increased their speed. They began to complain among themselves, especially since most were wearing black suits which made the heat unbearable.

The driver was not deterred by their complaints. His mind was now fully focused on Gosse's Tavern. Near Forest Road he whipped the horse again and she broke into a trot. By now the men in the procession were running to keep up with the horse. A lot of angry words were exchanged at graveside. When the funeral ended the mourners walked back to Jimmy Martin's to complain about the driver's conduct. Needless to say, Jimmy gave an apology and the driver was fired.

I recall another incident in which I teamed up with Spuds to cause a bit of an uproar at a wake taking place in a neighbours house. We both had listened attentively to Spuds' mother telling stories of her mischievous pranks when growing up in an outport community. One such prank involved putting pepper on a hot stove during a wake. We decided to try it. We both got a handful of pepper from our respective kitchen cupboards and went into the house to pay our respects.

The deceased, an elderly lady, was being waked in a front room of the house. That room and hallway was filled to capacity. We went to the kitchen and awaited the opportunity to drop the pepper. That chance came when the two women sitting at the kitchen table left the room. We quickly disposed of the pepper by tossing it over the top of the stove. We made a swift departure from the house.

The heat from the stove burned the pepper, producing a misty vapour to rise and spread throughout the house. When inhaled this would cause a burning sensation in the eyes and a spate of sneezing and coughing. We heard that sneezing and coughing coming from inside the house, then the front door opened and the mourners poured out into the street.

The fumes even penetrated the home of a neighbour who suffered from asthma. This lady could be seen with her head extended through an open window, coughing and gasping for breath. When the mist cleared the mourners returned completely mystified as to what happened. For years after those who were in the home that night speculated as to what caused the ghastly vapour which forced them into the street. Some even attributed the mystery to supernatural causes.

Many of the older downtown houses were bug infested and these caused special problems, particularly in the summer heat. I recall hearing of a harrowing incident that happened during a wake in a very dilapidated house on New Gower Street near City Hall. It was during a hot spell in July and the family were forced to ask everyone to leave the house and close the casket. The heat had caused the bugs to come out in force. They swarmed inside the coffin and over the deceased. Bug infestation was a problem in the older parts of town. It may have been a more widespread problem in the 1930s than the 40s. One gentleman told me of an effective way he used to prevent the bugs from getting into beds. They would immerse each of the four bed posts into a can partially filled with kerosene. Bugs trying to crawl into a bed would end up in the kerosene. I don't know if this was a widespread remedy, but it was certainly a remedy that was used by some.

A major housing program soon after Confederation wiped out some of the worst housing conditions this province has ever seen and moved the people to newly built subsidized housing units. The poor economic circumstances preceding Confederation forced people to rent flats wherever they could find one. We had no public housing at the time and wages were very low.

When the practice of waking people in a funeral home was initiated it was accepted reluctantly by most people who wanted to hang on to the old traditions. One of the reasons for the opposition was that people had trouble accepting that the funeral homes closed their doors at 10 p.m. leaving the corpse alone. In time, this opposition disappeared so that today, the practice of waking at home is practically unheard-of.

An old Harbour Scene—This photo shows the St. John's Harbour near the Murray premises as it looked during the early 1950s.

Chaytor's Butcher Store, on New Gower Street near the intersection at Casey Street and New Gower Street.

A Village Atmosphere

Gathering groceries to feed a family was far more complicated in those days. There were no convenient one-stop shopping supermarkets with their vast varieties to choose from. Our food menu was mainly meat and potatoes, or, on Wednesdays and Fridays, fish and potatoes.

These were the days when a woman's place was in the home. The job of taking care of a family was a full time job. The food needs of a family were gathered from several sources. First, the most reliable was the corner grocery store. Every neighbourhood had at least one and most had several. In the Flower Hill area there were Fardy's, Daddy Roberts, Duff's, Mike O'Keefe's, McGrath's, King's, Mike Williams, Hickey's, and Edney's to name a few. Some of these stores were convenience stores; others were grocery stores. Several times a week the owner would sprinkle the floor with sawdust or Dustbane and leave it there to absorb dirt and often the drippings from the large barrels of salt beef. Customers would regularly use a metal pick to sort out the meats in the barrel in search of a lean piece of meat.

Everybody had a charge account at the corner grocery stores. As kids we would go to Jim Fardy's store on Flower

Hill to buy a bottle of beer (soft drink or pop) and sit on a bundle of splits in the corner to drink it. 'Mark it down, Jim' would be heard over and over again as customers picked up items to go on their charge account at the store.

Jim Fardy generally knew everyone in the neighbourhood and when anyone told him to "Mark it down", he would know whose account was to be charged. However, I recall well an occasion when Patricia (Trish) Murphy, the youngest child in a large family, was just old enough to get out around the street to play with the other kids. Jim knew she was a neighbourhood child but had not yet learned her last name. Trish came into the store one day and asked for a roll of toilet paper. When Jim passed it to her she told him to, "Mark it down."

"Who is it for?" Jim asked Trish. She turned as she left the store and said, "It's for all of us." I never heard Jim Fardy laugh so heartily before or after.

Jim never missed an opportunity to inject humour or wit into a situation. One day a half dozen or so people were exchanging a lot of small talk as Jim tried to fill their orders. The conversation turned to the problem of being overweight. Paddy Murphy was a typical jolly overweight individual. While the women expressed opinions on the problems of being 'fat' Paddy pinched his midsection and commented, "This is not fat. My Doctor told me it's just water retention." Jim, who had been quietly listening to the exchange, leaned over the counter and shook Paddy's hand, saying, "Well how do you do, Bay Bulls Big Pond!"

Paddy Murphy also had a keen Irish wit that was shared by his brothers Mike and Ank. He would brighten the mood in a room just by his presence. On one occasion at Fardy's Store several men and women were standing around chatting and joking with one another. The widow Snow poked her finger into Paddy's stomach and said, "If this were a nail I could let all the air out of your stomach and you would look like a real man." Without hesitation Paddy retorted, "And you could use the air to pump up your chest so you could look like a real woman." Of course the exchange of barbs and insults was always good natured fun.

Households had no fridges or deep freezes to store meats and perishables. People would write down a list of their basic needs: canned goods, soaps, detergents etc. These lists would be left at the grocery store. All day Friday and Saturday the store owners would be busy filling the orders and there was usually a delivery boy to deliver the boxes of groceries. These delivery boys had specially built bicycles with a carrying basket on front in which a box of groceries could be deposited. A parcel carrier was also attached to the rear of the bicycle over the back wheel. This contraption had a spring controlled metal bar which snapped down over the item being delivered to prevent it from falling.

There were many farmers from the little villages around St. John's who carried on a profitable business of selling vegetables from door to door. The little horse-drawn carts loaded up with potatoes, cabbages, carrots, beets and berries of all kinds when in season. One lady who serviced the Flower Hill neighbourhood for years was a Mrs. Squires from St. Phillips. She had regular customers to supply. The 'meat man' also had regular visits and customers. A Mr. Porter from Fox Trap could be depended on to tie up his horse at the corner of Flower Hill and Central Street every Saturday. As a matter of fact Saturday was a busy day on Flower Hill. I have pleasant memories of the unpaved, dusty hill being a beehive of activity sparked by these vendors' visits to town. Up and down and on both sides of the hill the little produce wagons would stop and tie their horses to one of the parade of electric poles that dotted the streets. News of who was selling what quickly spread by word of mouth, and women came out of their houses to line up to buy their supply of vegetables or meat for Sunday dinner.

The weekly neighbourhood peddling by the vegetable and meat vendors introduced many of us to the variance in the way our fellow Newfoundlanders spoke the Queen's English. We were not used to hearing people drop their h's or put h's on where there were none. Occasionally some incident would accentuate these differences in speech, such as the one involving the meat man who came every Saturday morning to Flower Hill selling fresh meat from the back of his wagon.

The widow Snow was a difficult lady to get along with. She was a constant source of complaints and arguments and most women in the neighbourhood avoided her as much as possible. She tried the patience of the meat man on many occasions. She always insisted on meat with no fat, and would balk over the prices. No matter how the meat man tried to please her she always responded with criticism.

We were standing nearby watching in amusement as the cranky widow badgered the meat man, who by then was exhausted from his door to door selling. "Too much fat! . . . too much bone! . . . too expensive!" She went on and on in endless haranguing of the obviously agitated meat vendor. In desperation, the vendor grabbed the parcel of meat from the widows hands and passed her back her dollar. He then locked the meat in the wagon and got up front to drive his horse away as the widow Snow continued her verbal abuse. The vendor turned to the widow and shouted, "Kiss me h'arse; Go on me 'arse I won't be out tomorrow." When we translated this, we realized he was telling the widow "Kiss me arse," and telling his horse, "Go on my horse, I won't be out tomorrow."

The meat man was so frequent a visitor to downtown streets that he got to know the people very well. Jack McDonald was a supervisor with Crosbie's on the waterfront. One day the meat man asked Jack if there was a chance he could get work with Crosbie's. Jack replied that, "It's a poor time of year to look for work with us. We're laying them off down there every day." The meat man thought about this for a minute then asked, "Can ya give me a job laying em off?"

A cooked meal of salt beef and cabbage was a must for Sundays. However, the door to door meat man was not the only source of meat supplies. There were dozens of meat markets spread throughout the City. Most of these had their own cattle stocks which grazed in fields both in and outside the city. Some of these included Caseys, Clarke's, Glasco's, Chaytor's and Lawlor's. Fifty cents could purchase enough fresh beef to feed a family of four.

There was an exceptionally big demand for fish, particularly on Friday's. Roman Catholics were not permitted to eat meat on Friday so for them fish was a must. Wednesday was also traditionally a "fish day."

West Enders went to the fish market set up by city fishermen at Steer's Cove. There were dozens of hastily constructed stalls from which the fishermen sold their catch to long line-ups of customers.

Fish sold from five cents to fifty cents each. Five cents would get you a small fish which could feed two people. A fifty cent fish was a very large cod big enough to feed a large family.

Most families sent a son or daughter to Steer's Cove to purchase the fish. It was a common sight during the summertime on Friday's to see gangs of boys making their way to the

Cove, then the return journey with each boy dragging a fish home. The fishermen kept a good supply of old newspapers which they used to wrap the fish.

The menu was of far less variety than is the case today. Fish and potatoes, often with drawn butter; fish cakes, fish stews, and fish and brewis were a main part of the weekly menu. Frying meat with potatoes and gravy; meat stews, salt beef and cabbage, pork and cabbage, pork chop dinners and soups of all kinds were also an important part of the family menu. Usually, you could predict what was for dinner on almost any day of the week. Fish, Wednesday and Friday; salt beef and cabbage on Sundays, and pea soup on Saturday. Saturday, pea soup day, was known as the Devil's birthday.

The taste of pea soup was enhanced when cooked with ham bones. On Saturday mornings there would be a line of kids outside the Peter Pan Company on the top of Lime Street which sold ham bones at ten cents a piece. It was a great disappointment to many households when the Peter Pan outlet was destroyed by fire in the mid-1950s.

Peter Pan Sales had burned down at least once before. It happened around 1950 at a time when the building was entirely constructed of wood. Soon after, the company set out to replace it with a new concrete structure on the same site. The place was a beehive of activity with an army of labourers, painters, carpenters and loads of construction material. It was inevitable that such a concentration of activity would attract the attention of young boys from the neighbourhood looking for some excitement on a summer afternoon.

The Peter Pan site was almost in the back garden of the Rumsey family on Lime Street. Entrance to the property was obtained through a laneway near the side of their house. Gerard Rumsey, then about six or seven years old had a front row view of the daily activity on the site. But having just a view wasn't enough. After all, it seemed that in addition to the site being a centre of construction activity it also became a playground for the neighbourhood children. It wasn't long before Gerard joined the others in exploring and seeking adventure.

A large barrel filled with water, which the construction workers used when mixing cement, attracted his attention. Gerard managed to get on top of the barrel, removed the covering and accidentally fell head first into the water. Gerard was not a swimmer and being submerged under water was a terrifying experience for him. The confined interior of the barrel made it impossible for him to turn himself around. He struggled pushing his arms from one side to the other of the barrel. But all he was doing was wearing himself down. The child was slowly drowning.

Ed Goobie, a teenage boy who lived on Cabot Street, heard the cry of someone who shouted that a child had fallen into the barrel. He rushed to the scene and grabbing Gerard by the ankles pulled him from the barrel of water. It was a blessing that so many people were around that afternoon. The incident also served to dampen Gerard's adventurous spirit for some time after.

For those who did not bake or who wanted a break from housework, bread and cakes were available at the corner stores. These were supplied from the many bakeries around town. There were Walsh's Bakery on Central Street; Mammy's on Alexander Street, McQuires O'Boy Bakery on Adelaide Street, Moores Bakery which moved from Brien Street to Hamilton Avenue, and East End Bakeries on the Hill o' Chips. Bakeries sold the cuttings left over after making cakes and buns, direct to the customer from a little bread shop set up inside the bakery. These "scraps," as they were called, sold for ten cents a paper bag full or one dollar a sack. The sack was a flour sack. This was a real bargain because after the cake scraps were eaten the flour sack could be used to make a variety of things. Mothers made pillow slips, bloomers, table cloths, and pease pudding bags. One family on Lime Street even used the sacks to tar their roof.

Like vegetables and meat, fresh milk was also delivered door to door as well as being available from the corner store. Milk came in half pint, pint and quart bottles. When you purchased a bottle of milk at a store you paid a deposit on the bottle which was refunded when the bottle was returned. However, instead of requesting the refund of the deposit you would request the grocer to refill the empty bottle, a practice which saved the consumer money. Several dairy farmers ran a door to door delivery service to the city. I remember a Mr. Kelly from Middle Cove servicing the Flower Hill area. He had a horse drawn wagon and would hire a neighbourhood boy to help him with the deliveries. In the early 1950s Stevie Fowler of Flower Hill worked with old Kelly. Steve got to see his first farm when working for Kelly. Kelly invited Steve for a weekend stay at his farm. The kids at Middle Cove quickly discovered that Stevie was not familiar with farms when Steve came running out of the woods claiming he had found a cow's nest. What he had come across were a dozen or so discarded milk bottles.

Molasses was sold from barrels, also known as puncheons. It was more widely used in those days than today. People used it on fresh home made bread, toutons, toffee apples, molasses candy,and even to sweeten their tea. The customer could bring his own container to the corner store and purchase a jug of molasses. Tea bags were unheard of. People steeped fresh tea in a tea pot. You would pour the tea into a cup partly filling it, depending on how strong you wanted the tea. To keep the loose tea leaves from pouring into the cup a tea strainer was used. This was a small scoop size wire mesh which fitted across the top of a cup and sifted out the leaves as the tea poured into the cup. Then you would add boiling hot water to the tea in the cup.

Pepsi and Coke were always available, but we had a variety of other soft drink products as well. I remember soft drinks—which in those days everyone called beer—selling for seven cents a bottle. Then they went up to eight cents a bottle. If you wanted to differentiate between alcoholic beverages and soft drinks you would refer to the alcoholic beverage as good beer and the soft drink as simply beer. The presence of Canadian and American troops here in the 1940s and 1950s eliminated the word "beer" to describe soft drinks. The memory of beer as a soft drink was emblazoned in my memory by one of the meat men who sold his goods from the corner of Central Street on Saturday mornings. When he finished his work he would drop into Jim Fardy's store for a snack. Jack Murphy, Bouncer Abbott, Richard Murphy and myself always made sure to be in the store when he took his

Outing at Maloney's Meadow, Mount Pearl (Commonwealth Avenue area today). Taken 1950. L-R: Jack Murphy, Maurice Fitzgerald, Jim Murphy, Betty Murphy, John Walsh, Jack Fitzgerald, Donna Murphy, Betty Anthony. Standing L-R: Bouncer Abbott, Frank Whelan and Richard 'Dickie' Murphy.

break. His accent sounded funny to us and we always broke up when he asked Fardy, "Give me a beer, a square and one of dem over dere." Of course, he was asking for a Spur, a raisin square and a candy.

Other popular drinks included Spur Cola, Royal Crown Cola, and the Royal Beverages. The Royal on Barter's Hill made Lime Rickey, Orange Crush, Ginger Ale, Lemonade and a Chocolate carbonated soft drink, unique to the Royal and quite popular. This was a carbonated drink which you had to shake well before drinking.

During the 1920s and 1930s many small stores sold home made candy and ice cream. By far the most popular of these was Power's Candy store located in one of a group of house-sized buildings on New Gower Street known as Andrew's range. Mrs. Power developed her own recipe for home style ice cream which she advertised as Perfection Ice Cream. In the 1930s she even issued a challenge in the local papers for anyone to make a better product. Power's little store survived until around 1961 or 1962. It was the last of the old time candy and ice cream parlours and was very popular among the children of the west end when I was growing up downtown.

Mrs. Power while still in her seventies was making home made candy and ice cream. When you opened the door to enter her quaint little store a little bell attached to the top of the door would jingle and either Mrs. Power or her son Fatty Power would come out to the store from a little kitchen at the rear. A large glass display case featured the best of Power's home made candy and fudges. She made several flavours of fudge which included strawberry, chocolate, and vanilla flavours. These would be sprinkled with a coating of shredded coconut. Her most famous product was the bull's eye, a small brown coloured candy made from molasses and some other ingredients. Many have tried to duplicate her ice cream and candy recipes without success.

I especially remember her home made ice cream. I remember eating five of them in succession one hot summer's day. I would have eaten another five if I had had the money. A specialty for which there would be a line up after Sunday's children's mass at St. Patrick's Church was Mrs. Power's ice cream floats. These were made simply by putting a scoop of her home made ice cream into a soda glass and covering with your favourite soft drink. A lime would make a lime float, orange an orange float and so on. Ice creams sold for seven cents. On St. Patrick's Day children lined up to buy green ice-cream and green fudge. Her St. Paddy's Day floats were very popular. Those were simply made by mixing green ice cream with a lime beverage. Mrs. Power's floats cost fifteen cents. Her bulls eyes were three for a cent and her fudge sold for a penny a piece.

It was the search for Mrs. Power's grandson Tyrone Power in the early 1950s that led to the plane crash that killed Joe Butler, one of the founders of VOCM. Butler, flying his own private plane from Quidi Vidi Lake, crashed on take off. He was setting out to do an aerial search of the Topsail Beach area where Power was last seen. A couple of days later search parties located the boy alive and well.

Alcoholic beverages of any sort could be purchased only from the BLC (Board of Liquor Control Stores) or the breweries. Each person had a liquor book and was permitted to purchase only two bottles of alcohol in any week. Many bootleggers operated around the city and they found a good market among the American soldiers stationed at Pepperrell. They also found the Americans a cheap source for supplies. Liquor could be purchased on the base at a fraction of the cost at the BLC. Often soldiers smuggled it off base and sold it on the black market in the City. A mild alcoholic beverage was, however, available over the counter of most corner stores. It was called Haig Ale. This drink sold well, especially on holidays or after hours when the liquor stores and breweries were closed.

Buying food and drink for the household was different in those days, but so were all aspects of housekeeping. The years immediately after Confederation were a time of change, especially for those who lived in the city's worst tenements. These were houses which had been built prior to the 1892 fire which destroyed most of the City. These were the homes torn down in the first stages of the Government's new housing program after Confederation. They were houses which were neither wind nor water proof. The paint had long worn off them and the clapboards were falling off. Most of them were overcrowded even by standards at that time. There were no bathrooms as we know them today. They had no running water. The night soil carts (used to collect raw sewerage each night) were still very active and necessary.

St. John's first public housing units were built at Westmount, in the Cashin Avenue area and Livingstone Street downtown. Among these was a widows complex off Cashin Avenue, then referred to as the Ebsary Estate. These were apartment buildings which were for the exclusive use of widows and their families. The first families to move in felt they were in the lap of luxury, since most had been moved from some of the worst tenements the city had to offer.

One new resident of the Widows' Complex found her surroundings hard to adapt to. There was plenty of room, and care was taken not to overcrowd people. The apartments were spacious and modern in every way with electricity, running water, and a modern bathroom with sink, toilet and a bathtub. One lady who was moved to this complex looked all round the apartment for a coal pound. She had been used to having one off her kitchen near her stove. She learned the coal pound was in the basement. Each building had a series of partioned stalls with individual locks in the basement which were used to store coal. This meant the widows or their children had to climb several flights of stairs each day to retrieve a bucket of coal for the kitchen stove. This became particularly burdensome in wintertime. This lady chose to use her bath as a coal storage area and consequently she filled the tub with coal.

This incident became common knowledge throughout the City and disgusted many people. Housing officials denied it, but I have verified that it did happen. However, living conditions at the time should be taken into consideration. This lady had done without a bathtub all her life. Like most people in the City, she used the traditional galvanized tub on the kitchen table on Saturday nights to bathe. To her the bathtub was a luxury. She still had the old family tub, but she found it burdensome in winter carrying buckets of coal up over several flights of stairs. So she did what made sense to her. She could get along without a bathtub, but not without coal.

Coal companies delivered the fuel by the quarter, half and full ton loads. Their horse drawn delivery carts would back in near the house and dump the load of coal. Most homes had a coal shute from the outside which allowed the coal to be shovelled straight into the coal pound in the basement. These were accessed through a small opening outside with a cover, usually locked, which measured about two feet square. Many of the older homes in town still have these openings but they are no longer needed.

Wood needed to ignite the coal fire was available from

door to door delivery men or from the corner stores. The stores always had a corner where the 'split man,' as he was called, would pile the wooden splits. These sold from ten to twenty-five cents a bundle. The need for splits also presented a business opportunity for the enterprising youngsters of the day. They would gather scraps of wood or chop up wood which they collected from a variety of sources and fill brin bags. These bags of wood were sold door to door for twenty-five to fifty cents a bag.

Coal stoves gave off a good heat and in the winter time the kitchen was the warmest place in a house. Many homes also had coal stoves in their hallways or parlours (front rooms). However, homes were usually very cold in winter and families relied on blankets and heavy quilts to keep warm while sleeping. Before going to bed the last one up would 'bank down the fire.' To do this you would take the coal shovel (a small shovel kept with a bucket of coal placed near the stove for convenience) and shovel ashes from the grate area which you would spread over the fire. This would cause the fire to smoulder throughout the night and slowed down the burning of the coal. Consequently, heat could be maintained in the kitchen throughout the night. This made it more comfortable for the first person into the kitchen in the morning. The kitchen still had some heat, and it was much easier to get a good fire going to cook breakfast.

The use of wood and coal was also a source of a lot of dust and dirt. The ashes left in the stove after the fire and the ashes that would fall from a grate into a catch-all would be shovelled out several times a week and placed into a bucket known as an 'ash-can' or 'ash-bucket.' These buckets of ash were put outside the house daily and picked up by the Ash-man, as the garbage man was called in those days. The term "garbage man" was rarely used and there was little in the way of garbage to be collected because people burned most of their trash.

Many men made their living working for coal companies. By the end of a day's work these men were literally black-faced, with grains of coal dust ingrained into their skin. The same was true of the longshoremen who unloaded the coal boats at the harbour. It was easy to tell who worked at coal in those days.

Soon after Confederation, oil stoves became the rage. At first people showed a fear of oil. Housewives feared that a house fire could easily result from its use. However, as people became aware of how safe and clean oil actually was, the old coal stoves soon disappeared. In place of coal pounds people now needed an oil barrel to store their stove oil and a place to store the barrel. While oil was not as messy as coal, it did leave an odour.

Sunlight soap was universally used to clean house, wash laundry, and bathe the family. Women used the soap to scrub their front steps. For some reason it seemed important that the front steps and windows had to be cleaned. It was a common sight on Saturdays to see women on hands and knees scrubbing the front step on a house.

Wash day, usually Mondays, was a true day of toil for the lady of the house. First, water had to be carried in buckets from the neighbourhood water tank. Children sometimes helped with this chore. To do a family wash, and have enough water for family needs for the day, required a series of trips to and from the water tank. On Flower Hill, the tank was located at the corner of Flower Hill and Central Street adjacent to the Cranshaw household. There was another water tank at the corner of Clifford Street and Stephen Street.

Every neighbourhood had its water tank. Once the water was in the house the housewife had to boil enough to fill a large aluminum wash tub. She would then proceed with the labour of washing the clothes by hand in the tub of hot water using lye soap or Sunlight Soap. A scrub board was used to manually scrub the dirt out of the clothes. This was a board of heavy ribbed glass with a wooden frame. The housewife would run the clothes item up and down over this repeatedly until all the dirt was out. Then she would ring the water out with her hands. When the task of washing and scrubbing was finished she would take the wet clothes to the back garden and hang the items on a line, using clothes pins. During winter months clotheslines were strung throughout the house and the clothing was dried inside the home.

Stella Reid remembers well the drudgery of wash days. Mrs. Reid lived on Sebastian Street and used two large iron boilers to heat water for the Monday clothes wash. But first she had to drag five and six buckets of water from the tank. She had an advantage over some others in the neighbourhood because she lived adjacent to the tank and did not have far to go. The detergents used were very harsh. Lye which was added to hot water had to be handled very cautiously. It was like an acid if it got on your hands or clothing in its pure state.

To clean white clothing, Mrs. Reid explained, "We used squares of 'Blue', the 'Blue' made whites whiter." When the water on the stove was hot enough, Mrs. Reid would lift it from the stove and pour it into a the same galvanized tub that was used as a bath tub on Saturdays. Mrs. Reid would then take the suds drenched clothing to the tank and run cold water through them to get the suds out. Then she would use her scrub board to further clean and get as much water out as possible. "When this was done," she recalled, "I would take the clothes to the back garden and hang them on the clothes line to dry. No such thing as electric washers and dryers in those days." Just keeping house was a full time job.

Personal hygiene was achieved with a wash pan, and the galvanized tub used for washing clothes, also served as the family bath tub. Three times a day, usually before each meal, family members would fill the wash pan, and wash their face and hands. A porcelain jug and bowl was also a common sight in households. The jug was kept filled with water for washing purposes.

Saturday night was the night for the tub. This was the one night of the week when kids had to go home early to get a bath. One by one they would be washed in the tub. The older children would have to wash themselves from the tub, while the smaller children were put in the tub and scrubbed clean by their mothers. After the scrubbing the fine tooth comb would be used to make sure your head was totally clean.

The nightsoil cart—better known as the "Honey Wagon"—was very much a part of life in St. John's up until the early 1950s, and their use in parts of the City lingered much longer. These carts operated in the dark of night. The nightsoil car was about the size of a pick-up truck and had a covered back. Two men operated each unit. They were often targets of young pranksters. A common joke played on these workers was to place a brick or large rock into a bucket of nightsoil. The boys would hide somewhere nearby to get a good view of the bucket being dumped. The cart would proceed down over the Hill stopping to pick up each bucket and dumping it into the wagon. When they dumped the bucket with the brick or rock the nightsoil would splatter all over the worker. The boys would then run all out, through gardens, over fences and laughing all the way. I don't recall any of them ever getting caught. To avoid being targeted with this type of mischief the more experienced collectors shook the bucket side to side before emptying it. This usually detected the presence of a brick, rock or some other heavy object.

Another prank involved the use of a long rope. The boys would tie the slop buckets, each to the one adjacent to it until they ran out of rope. To get the most buckets possible they would combine several ropes together. When the honey wagon appeared on a street they would pull the rope causing all the buckets to tip over. It was far more difficult to get away with this sort of prank because it affected everyone on the street. Men would come out of their houses to put a stop to the prank, or if they caught up with the pranksters they would forcibly escort them home where punishment usually awaited.

A story was often told of the honey wagon driver who lost his coat in the night soil. He had placed the coat on the cover of the wagon, and it accidentally fell into the nightsoil. The man extended his hand into the mess to retrieve it. Mrs. Tobin, who was on her door steps shouted to him, "You're not going to wear that now?' He replied, "Not bloody likely. I just wanted to get my lunch back. I had it in my coat pocket."

Every street had a hopper which people sometimes used to empty their slop buckets. A hopper was a square hole in the ground with a pipe outlet connecting with the St. John's Harbour. These were covered with a square contraption of iron made up of iron bars separated about two inches from each other. They were called gratens. While this may have been common in the early 1940s it was not so common in my time. I do remember however, seeing evidence that one or two of the hoppers that some were still used for disposing of slop. In my area people used it to dump the remains of a cooked dinner, or dirty water on wash day. The streets had a drain running down on each side made of a semi-circular length of concrete and sandstone. People used these drains to dump liquids which would run down to the hoppers.

In the 1950s the nightsoil carts were still dumping the slops in a sewer collection site at the top of Adelaide Street adjacent to Livingstone Street. This was a concrete building with direct pipe connection to the harbour.

No house or rented "flat," as we called apartments then, was without a couch or a day bed in the kitchen. Couches were covered with leather or imitation leather. Which type you had depended on how much you could afford to spend. The imitation leather was the predominant one in use. These couches were shaped in such a way to include a raised head rest. They were a necessary part of kitchen furniture because they provided a temporary resting place for the housewife who after hours of working in the kitchen often wanted and needed a rest period. Day beds, on the other hand, were frequently used in the kitchen to relieve overcrowding. Many people used a double day bed. At night these folded out from a single unit to a double bed. In the morning, they were fold-back into a single unit and served as a couch or resting place during the day-time.

Those couches lasted a lifetime! When the covering wore out people would pay a visit to Elsie Heale's at 114 Casey Street. Elsie and her sister operated a dry goods store there and knew almost everyone in the area by first name. Shopping at Elsie's was like dropping in on a relative or old friend.

As people prospered in the 1950s these couches and day beds were often sent to the dump or sold to American antique collectors. They became relics of the past because there was no place in a modern home for a couch or day bed. Overcrowded bedrooms gave way to each family member having a bedroom or sharing with only one other person.

The main drags in the city were Water Street, New Gower

Street (sometimes called Middle Street) and LeMarchant Road. New Gower and LeMarchant Road had many small candy and soda shops or Fish n' Chip stores where people stopped for refreshments. A popular one on New Gower Street was the Chicken Coup. There were many Chinese restaurants as well along New Gower and Water Street. We had no shopping malls or Trans Canada Highway in those days. Before television, people—especially in mild and warm weather—went for evening walks on one of these streets. Frequently, whole families strolled the streets together. In addition to our local people the streets were crowded with soldiers from the American bases at Pleasantvile and Argentia. The 'Yanks' strolled the streets looking for 'a land.' A land was a common phrase to describe getting a date. Both male and females would refer to going for a walk to catch 'a land.'

Taverns were the exclusive watering holes for men. Whether the women were barred by law, or chose to avoid such places because of custom and tradition I do not know. Anyway, the taverns of the City were male sanctuaries where the men could drink and be themselves away from the judgemental eye and sharp tongue of a disapproving wife. Yet, ironically, visiting or dropping into a tavern for a nip was the source of disorder in many households.

Friday was the traditional weekly pay day for most people in town. Many workers cashed their cheques or opened their pay envelopes to take money from their wages for a few beers at the neighbourhood tavern before the wife got her hands on it. Spending money from the weekly pay cheque before bringing it home was a cardinal sin in the eyes of the housewife, who laboured all week caring for the family and patiently awaited the arrival of the husband's pay to pay bills and manage the household. Then there was the added burden of trying to deal with the husband who drank too much and spent too much.

In those days taverns closed at 10:00 p.m. Those who imbibed too long would end up staggering up over the hills and streets trying their best to walk straight, but without success. I recall seeing many a working man sitting on a doorstep waiting for the strength to go further or the courage to go home and face the wife. From the man's viewpoint, a visit to the tavern was well deserved. The men worked all week—in many cases a six day week—for low wages and by the weekend needed to unwind and relax in the company of friends. But paydays were stressful times for many households. After the taverns closed on Friday and Saturday nights the Black Mariah had its work cut out.

For some reason the most popular song among the drinking workers of the City was, "I belong to Glasgow." They would sing it together in the tavern, hum it walking home and roar it out at home to drown out the wife's tongue lashing, which was inevitable under the circumstances. It was not at all unusual to see an impatient housewife waiting outside a tavern or standing in the doorway of a tavern beckoning her husband to come out. I recall watching one lady sending her young son inside the tavern to get the father to come out. She grabbed a couple of *Evening Telegram*'s and told the young boy to go inside and pretend to be selling the paper. She told him that if he saw his father in there to send him right out. He did see his dad and told him, "Mom wants you out by the door." When the husband emerged through the front door, she grabbed him by the collar and dragged him all the way up to their home on Codner's Lane.

Some men avoided the taverns and purchased their own beer or rum to take home. A 'pup' of rum was smaller than a flask and many a longshoreman managed to smuggle one onto his job site.

Before container ships were introduced there was always plenty of work on the waterfront for longshoremen. You had to be a union member, however, in order to get that work. Every morning hundreds of men would line up at the different wharves. As jobs became available the supervisor would call out a person's name and that man would take his position working with others in loading or unloading the cargo ships. Sometimes, when things were slow, these jobs were very competitive. On one occasion two men from the Flower Hill area were in the same line up waiting for work. When the supervisor, Andy Samuelson, called "Tom" (not his real name) to step forward for a job his friend "Mike" (also not his real name) shouted, "That's not fair. I got seven kids at home." Tom, with three children himself and known for his forthright opinions and wit, shouted back, "What do ya think I got home, Mike . . . ducks?" Mike and Tom had many such encounters but it never affected their friendship.

Working longshore had its perks. Tom once swiped a box of sneakers which he proudly brought home to his young school age boys. "Here's enough sneakers to do ye a lifetime," he said as he emptied the box onto the kitchen floor. The boy's enthusiasm soon waned when they discovered the sneakers were all the same size—elevens—and all for the left foot. When they complained Tom told them, "Wear'em to school anyway. Just cross your legs when ya sit down and the brother won't know the difference."

Water Street was the main and only shopping centre in town. The major department stores granted credit to families to purchase family clothing and other household needs. The limit varied and the payments were low. However, the collection of accounts was handled very differently than is the case in modern times. Each store had a bill collector who went door to door in the neighbourhoods collecting the weekly payments. The collector for the Royal Stores was a gentleman who lived in our area and was very well liked and respected by everyone.

Fred Candow—a prominent member of the CLB Band for several decades—went door to door with a black leather folder containing the official receipt book and a pouch to store the payments received. People paid whatever they could afford and payments usually ranged from fifty cents to five dollars weekly. Fred got to know most families and his visits became more like social visits for his customers. He would be invited in for a cup of tea or people would chat with him about the events of the day.

Brazil Square, right in the heart of centre town, was distinctly different from other streets. That was because it was predominantly comprised of boarding houses. These houses were always filled to capacity. Out of town taxis were constantly coming and going as they picked up or dropped off passengers at the boarding homes. Some of these houses were called: The Four Star Boarding House; Eddy's boarding House; Emberley's Boarding House; Mercer's Boarding House and the Brownsdale Hotel. A much larger house than the others, the Brownsdale was actually on the corner of Brazil Square and New Gower Street.

Weddings were frequently held in houses. Just as they did for wakes, families cleared the kitchen and one or two other rooms to accommodate the guests. If the family had no record player a neighbour would always supply one. Neighbours loaned chairs, dishes and records to the family hosting the wedding celebration. That was the case when Ron Gollop and Dolores Murphy married. The wedding was held at the Murphy's house on Flower Hill. That was 1958, and Ron and

Dolores are still happily married today almost forty years later. Bill Bennett and Marjorie Evoy married in the mid 1940s and held their wedding at a friend's flat at a home on the corner of Notre Dame Street. Bill served overseas in WWII and remained in the Canadian Army until his retirement in the late 1960s.

While children read and traded comic books during this era the adults did the same with pocket books and magazines. Zane Grey's Westerns were very popular. Dago Janes often traded books with Jimmy Hearn who lived on Flower Hill at the time. Jimmy was well liked by everyone but was never hesitant to let his feelings be known. There were no back doors with Jimmy. What he had to say was said to your face, "like it or lump it." It was this trait in Jimmy's personality that probably endeared him to his friends and neighbours. Dago was also liked and known for some wild escapades like swimming across the Harbour or carrying a steel garbage can in his teeth across Flower Hill. But Dago made one too many trips to Jimmy's door to borrow books.

About 3:00 a.m. one day Jimmy was awakened by a knocking on his door. He came down the stairs from his second flat bedroom to answer the door. Meanwhile, Dago had been pounding hard on the door hoping to get an answer. When he opened the door Dago immediately made his pitch. "Sorry, to get you up Jimmy. I'm awake the whole night and can't get to sleep. How about a few books?"

Jimmy said, "Can't sleep eh! I got just the thing for you." Jimmy disappeared into the kitchen while Dago had stepped into the hall to wait. Moments later Jimmy appeared again. "This will help you sleep," he said, as he popped Dago over the head with a frying pan. Jimmy closed the door and went back to bed. Dago walked wobbly-legged back to his house.

In later years I had the honour of acting as master of

The first Belmont Tavern was located on New Gower Street east of Barron Street. Before being converted into a tavern this was the site of the old Ritz Movie Theatre.

ceremonies at a number of downtown weddings and social events. People loved stories of the old neighbourhood and had an extraordinary interest in humorous stories which had a connection with city life in the 1940s and 1950s. One particular story depicting the village type atmosphere of the town in that era always sparked hilarity.

When Ned Hickey passed away a funeral mass was held at St. Patrick's Church. Ned left a wife and two daughters. In those days everyone knew everyone else. If you didn't know a person by name you knew them by sight. The Hickeys were very well liked and on the day of the funeral St. Patrick's Church was filled to capacity with standing room only.

Celebrating the funeral mass were Father Power and Father Bradshaw. Father Power was a very gentle soft-spoken man, whose tone of voice was a couple of decibels above a whisper. Father Bradshaw was hard of hearing and spoke loudly. Most people didn't like going to confession to Father Bradshaw because you were ex-

Walsh's Bakery, Central Street.

pected to talk louder than usual. He spoke loudly as well, so it was easy to hear the confessional conversation outside the confessional box.

Well, after everyone had taken their seats Father Power noticed that Mrs. Hickey and her two daughters had just entered the church walking behind the casket. He looked around the church and determined there were no vacant seats. He leaned a little towards Father Bradshaw and whispered, "Get three chairs for the Hickeys."

"What did you say, Father?" asked Father Bradshaw.

Speaking a little louder Father Power again asked, "Get three chairs for the Hickeys."

"I'm sorry, you'll have to speak up, Father, I can't hear you," answered Father Bradshaw.

Irritated by his failure to move Father Bradshaw to action, Father Power took a deep breath and in his loudest voice shouted towards Father Bradshaw, "Three . . . chairs . . . for the Hickeys."

Everyone in church stood up and responded: "Hip, hip hooray!, Hip hip hooray! Hip hip hooray!

When I was a boy a poem often recited at family gatherings was entitled **Those Were The Days.** Thanks to the late Frank "Spotty" Baird who kept a copy I am able to pass it onto you.

> *Do you remember when*
> *say thirty-forty years*
> *you never saw your sweetheart's limbs,*
> *but judged her by her ears.*
> *The kids were washed on Saturday night*
> *their daddy cut their hair,*
> *their suit was made from uncle's pants,*
> *and they wore no underwear?*

The women padded, but did not paint,
nor smoke, nor drink, nor vote.
@POEM = *The men wore boots and little stiff hats,*
and whiskers like a goat.
Not a soul had appendicitis
nor thought of buying glands
The butcher gave his liver away
but charged you for his hams.
You never needed a bank account
your beer gave six per cent
the hired girl got three bucks a week
and 12 bones paid the rent.
You could stand each night when work was o'er
with one foot on the rail
and your hip supported not a thing
except your own shirt tail.
You had real friends and trusted them,
You knew they were sincere
Those were the happy, joyous days
we wish they'd again appear.
(from Ghosts Heroes and Oddities,
Jack Fitzgerald, Jesperson Press,1991.)

The phrase "Those were the days," is enough said to indicate the regard people had for the City and its people during the era covered in this book. They were difficult and challenging times, but unlike today people pulled together and were their brothers' keepers. It was the very different society that has left those of us who experienced life in St. John's in that era with wonderful, happy, golden memories of a lifestyle that has been lost forever.

City of St. John's Archives — C1079 11.02.048

Part of the old neighbourhood — This photo shows Marty's Take-Out restaurant, the Jim Gay Laundry and Chaytor's Butcher store. Taken on Duckworth Street near the Casey Street intersection.